# Brown Water

## A Narrative of My Personal Journey in the Wake of Lewis and Clark

## Butch "Mr. Keelboat" Bouvier
## Onawa, Iowa

*Butch Bouvier 2022*

BROWN WATER
A Narrative of My Personal Journey in the Wake of Lewis and Clark

Cover photo by Butch Bouvier

ISBN: 978-0-692-43704-9

Printed in U.S.A.

*To my best friend and confidant for over forty-seven years,*
*the one who stood by my side, led the way,*
*or sometimes pushed from behind to get me to follow my crazy dreams—*
*my wife, and still my bride, Catherine,*
*who put up with more than anyone could ever know.*


*To my father, Alfred C. Bouvier Sr.*
*He lived life his way, and showed me how to do it also.*


*To my dear friend, Dick Hawes,*
*who taught me what he did by being who he was.*

# Contents

# Acknowledgments

OK, folks, since this is not the Oscars, and *no one* is going to start playing music before I'm done, I hopefully will not forget anyone. If you helped at all with this endeavor and ever wanted to see your name in a book, here's your chance! If you are not interested, I would suggest you just roll right past this section.

First I have to acknowledge my daughter, Shari Bouvier (my second-born and my favorite). She was invaluable to making this manuscript as good as it could be, with me being stubborn about not changing my words. I bet she spent as many hours rewriting and editing as I did scribbling it down.

The next person who finally made this happen is my wife, Catherine, who kept building a fire under me to keep going, and spent many hours editing.

And my good friends, Richard and Sandy Hawes, put the final piece of the puzzle in place when they convinced me I could self-publish.

Many other folks helped by proofreading and cheering me on. I hope I get them all listed: Wendy Bouvier (my first-born and my favorite), Marylyn Hawes, Brad Holder, Kira Gale, Jackie Warnstadt, and Bruce Narveson.

I also especially wish to thank Charles Wood II for his enthusiasm and support of this project, and Becky Lowe-Weyand, who provided editorial expertise and book formatting. You two helped my dream finally come true!

# Preface

Sailing ships have been carrying goods, materials, and people from one continent to another for hundreds of years. The deep-blue oceans of this world have always been highways of commerce and exploration. These blue-water fleets of well-documented sailing vessels have sparked our imaginations and have been the subject of countless books, paintings, and legends.

Almost forgotten to history are the water highways that crisscross every landmass on earth. These streams, lakes, and rivers were the transportation and exploration roads primarily used prior to the twentieth century. Since the advent of railroads and improved highways and road systems, these waterways, although still used for commerce, have lost their dominance in the area of transporting people.

The steamboat experienced a well-documented and glorified romantic age on our American inland waterways for most of the nineteenth and part of the early twentieth centuries. Prior to that time, hearty men conquered these waters in wooden boats. These craft were distinctively designed and constructed for shallow inland waters, and were powered only by manpower and the wind. The pre-steam era on our inland waterways is the lost child of time. The pioneers of the West could not spend a lot of time documenting their travels by boat; they just did it! Fighting changing channels, swollen rivers choked with debris, and muddy water, these brown-water rivermen opened up our fledgling waterways for the great steamboaters to follow.

In this book, I will cover some of our lost history, and techniques developed by the brown-water rivermen who pioneered inland waterway travel in the seventeenth and eighteenth centuries in America. I hope you will come to better understand the fundamental differences between ocean, or "blue-water" craft, and inland waterways, or "brown-water" craft, as we travel together through these little history lessons along that timeless river called the Missouri. I will place special emphasis on the boats of the Lewis and Clark Expedition of 1804–1806.

I have always used a Socratic approach when sharing my historical research, and this book will not detour from that path. I will share some history "puzzle pieces" with you. But if you are expecting more answers than questions, you may be disappointed. You will, however, encounter some very interesting points. I will raise questions and share with you my convictions about the rivercraft of the Lewis and Clark Expedition. This book is intended to stimulate you, and let you think for yourself. And I hope you'll have a fun time doing it! If you'd like to be challenged to think for yourselves, if you'd like to be presented with some very interesting information, if you'd like to experience some of my adventures while having a few good laughs, then please read on. I sincerely hope that you enjoy my efforts. Thank you.

## Disclaimer

As I began to assemble my thirteen-year compilation of short stories, journals, and notes, I realized that it would probably be wise to contact all the people mentioned in the book—to let them know that my long effort was almost complete, and to get their permission, once again, to use their names and their written journals. When I had asked them to keep journals, I made it clear that my hopes were to publish them some day. I always have and will continue to do as much of my business on a handshake as I can. In this day and age of zeal for legal action simply because some coffee was too hot, though, it seemed prudent to get written permission to reprint the journals.

When I set out to contact all who were included in my book, I soon found out I was facing a daunting task. There are so many people involved in my life's adventures. Heck! I couldn't even locate some of them. So I have decided to handle it in this way: If I have consent, I will use first and last names. If I do not have permission, I will only use first names, and I will attempt to remove anything that would identify them. Furthermore, I can tell you for a fact that I wouldn't choose to use someone's name—first, last, or otherwise—in my life story if I didn't respect the person.

# The Boats of the Lewis and Clark Expedition

## Through the Eyes of a Boatbuilder:
## A Question of Accuracy

I am a researcher and builder of eighteenth- and nineteenth-century American rivercraft. I have been studying boats and boat construction for over forty years. Since 1985, I have been primarily focused on the craft of the Lewis and Clark Expedition. In fact, my key interest in the expedition has always been the boats. Through unavoidable osmosis, however, I have picked up quite a bit on the subject of the day-to-day activities of the Lewis and Clark Expedition.

As an avid woodworker, I have built wooden boats since the late-1960s, my attention being drawn to early-American rivercraft in the mid-1980s. My devotion to these pre-steam era inland watercraft eventually led me into a career. In the year 2000, I founded L&C Replicas, which is "Dedicated to the research, restoration, and replication of the inland watercraft, machinery, and other structures of our past, so that we may better understand the role each played in our history." I have designed and built more Lewis and Clark Expedition boats than anyone else in the country. They range from functioning, full-scale replicas to quarter-scale models.

I see myself as a "hands-on" historian with a passion for living history. I have researched and studied the available written material on the Lewis and Clark Expedition at great length. I have also operated replicas of the rivercraft used in the Lewis and Clark Expedition…on the same river and in the same manner as they described in their journals. Throughout my experiences, I've kept meticulous notes about the boats. I've made observations and proposed theories, which have led me to conduct numerous experiments, in order to shed some light on the boats used by the men of this historical expedition.

It has become apparent to me that no one else has looked at these craft through the eyes of a professional wooden boatbuilder. I am aware of a proliferation of misleading information and have been disappointed or appalled by what has been written concerning the craft of the Lewis and Clark Expedition. There have been so many wild conclusions drawn about the boats that I fear that the truth, if it were out there to be found, has been all but lost.

Well-meaning authors have written books on this subject who know nothing of building these craft, let alone have experience running them on a river as expedition members would have. Often an author's source material is written by other authors who are equally crippled by ignorance of the boats themselves. These well-intentioned authors don't know a mooring bit from a thole pin. Some model boatbuilders have never built anything weighing over a pound or two, let alone twelve tons! These factors have all steered the subject of early-American, pre-steam era rivercraft into a whirlpool of confusion!

One of the problems with the literature about the Lewis and Clark Expedition is the way in which quotes from the expedition journals are used. In order for a quote to be accurate, it must be a full and complete quote, taken in context. Otherwise, its true meaning is compromised. For example, an author may include as a quote from the journals, "We proceeded on up this new branch, all men rowing." When the full quote as it appears in the journals reads, "We proceeded on up this new branch with all men at their stations." Are we then to assume that the men's stations were rowing stations? The enthusiastic author has made the assumption that the term *stations* automatically means *rowing stations*. Maybe stations is a general term used by the journalist meaning that all men were at their appointed positions on the boat, manning ropes, push-poling, and so on.

You may think this a picky little point, but it could lead to a general misconception of the events being described by the original journalist. You need to constantly go back to your source material to keep your assumptions in check. It's perfectly all right to make assumptions about historical events or documentation, if you make it clear that they are just that—assumptions. Without this disclaimer, you are misleading the reader and disturbing the interpretation of the historical event or document.

I will note here, that in this book, when I quote or reference the journals, I am using the three Lewis and Clark Expedition "bibles," as I call them. (I am also using a nautical dictionary from the 1800s.) These are considered primary source materials for gleaning information regarding the Lewis and Clark Expedition. They are:

The Definitive Journals of Lewis and Clark, edited by Gary E. Moulton
Letters of the Lewis and Clark Expedition, edited by Donald Jackson
A Journey Through the West: Thomas Rodney's 1803 Journal from Delaware
    to the Mississippi Territory, edited by Dwight L. Smith and Ray Swick
The Mariner's Dictionary, by Gershom Bradford

## Some questions we should be asking

Sadly, Hollywood generally does not help in the quest for historical accuracy. One motion picture oddity is the fascination with filming people walking in the water. My crews have not shared that fascination. We have been grounded many times, and all efforts are made with poles and oars before anyone even suggests getting into the water (unless the urgency of the moment prompts a quick decision). Even then, it is not a "mass exodus" over the side. Jumping overboard may be dramatic, but it is also very dangerous. The Missouri of 1804 was a muddy, snag-infested monster, which was destined to become one of the most important water highways in this country. I have heard it said that finding the Missouri River was like finding a wonderful wild mountain lion in your basement. How do you tame it safely?

Wading in a wild, muddy river is very dangerous any time, whether now or in 1804. We read of people drowning in the Missouri every year, and as often as not, they were just wading along the shallows. These shallows hide holes, which once you're sucked into, you most often do not get out of, as they are already full of debris, which entombs you. Around where I live, the locals call the Missouri the Muddy MO. The men of the Lewis and Clark Expedition considered it too thick to drink but too thin to plow. If there were a decent bank to walk on, I am confident they would use it. When there was no bank, they did walk in the water, but it was not their first choice.

Now when you're chest-deep in the river, you have to feel your way along the bottom. This takes a certain amount of effort just to move your legs forward and feel for solid footing safely. And, oh, did I mention the additional factors of a five-to seven-mile-per-hour current and who knows what other debris that's floating in the water? Now grab a rope with a nine-to ten-ton boat attached to it! (Don't forget to figure in the twelve to fifteen tons of supplies onboard.) Are we having fun yet?

How about those dramatic Hollywood movie scenes where the mountain men are pulling that dugout or canoe against the mountain stream with a decent bank to walk on within view? When it comes to mountain streams, they are generally not very deep, and usually pretty clean, but they are filled with rushing water, and they're cold as hell! Have you ever tried to stand on moss-covered stones…in moccasins? Could you keep your footing if the water were hitting you at mid-calf or higher at about thirty miles per hour? Have you ever heard of hypothermia!? I'm not saying these actions were never attempted. I'm confident they probably were, but I am willing to bet that these actions were only attempted when they had to be, and when there was no other way! Both common sense and my personal experiences tell me that the men of the Lewis and Clark Expedition would have sought out the path of least resistance, just as my crewmembers have over the years whenever they could. The next time you see a movie with men splashing about in the river less than ten feet from a nice shoreline, please ask yourself some common sense questions about the scene in front of you.

Human nature has not changed since the first man walked this earth, neither have the physical properties of wood. Another anomaly I've seen is the way artists depict the keelboat, or I should say barge. (We'll get into that later.) I guess they've invented rubber wood that will bend any way you want it to. Rubber wood…that's a neat idea! Now I can tell you that with steam you can get a wooden plank to bend quite a lot, but generally it severely resists being bent in two directions. You might get her to stretch a little along her width, but not as much as some artists depict. A wood plank will bend in a pretty predictable manner. A professional woodworker can spot one that is acting unnaturally very quickly. Of course, nowadays, when you're working with plywood, fiberglass, and metal, you can do as you please. But as an 1800s boatwright would tell you, when you're working with a good ol' green plank of oak, you will pretty much do as it wants!

We know from journal entries that the oars (and also, more likely than not, push-poles) were "slung" from the sides of the cabin. Through experimentation, I have found that storing them in a rope sling, just above the cabin windows, works very well. A couple of talented, well-meaning artists (who lack on-river experience) show some nice wooden brackets, just above the cabin windows, to store the oars on. I can tell you for a fact that when these types of brackets are pinned between a twelve-ton boat and a high riverbank or overhanging tree limb, they get destroyed, and your oars end up floating downstream. I have experimented with my rope slings verses solid brackets. My crew and I found (after we scraped down the bank and broke a few tree limbs) that the rope theory seemed very plausible. Why, you ask? Well, once past the encounter with the riverbank and falling branch debris, we looked back, and we still had our oars!

In one depiction of the keelboat/barge, its yard and reefed sail is raised and stowed high on the very top of the mast. This may look nice in a picture, but I've learned this: as long as the yard is high enough to walk under, it's plenty high enough! The higher you place your weight on a boat, the greater it negatively affects the critical center of gravity and the overall stability of the craft. Placing it high only heightens your risk amid strong, gusty winds, or when wheeling onto a sandbar. **Placing the yard so low on the mast that you cannot walk under it is another dumb oversight.** At any given time on a moving body of water, you may have to get from one end of the boat to another quickly, and having an obstacle like a yard in your way could be disastrous.

Historical research can be like the assembly of an intricate puzzle. Each piece possesses its own unique variables, but when all the pieces are finally in place, each has played its critical part in recreating an entire picture. The only difference is that a puzzle usually has a key—say, a picture on the lid of the box. All you need to do is locate all the pieces, group them, and study them a bit. And then you begin putting them into their proper places to recreate the complete picture. With historical research, you're trying to accomplish the same thing, but the lid to your box is either missing or only partially there! Sometimes, you will stumble upon a Rosetta Stone of sorts, but as often as not you're still left with questions to resolve. We are going to take this history puzzle in particular and apply my hands-on living history experiments to help recreate a picture and prove theories, which will lead to more accurate assumptions.

Throughout the years, I've kept thousands of notes and pictures pertaining to the Lewis and Clark craft. I've written and collected short narratives of my adventures relating to experiments with my replica boats. I continue to compile my eclectic assortment of written documents concerning the things I have learned, questioned, and challenged. I have two phrases in particular that I gravitate toward when conducting living history research and integrating it with the information I've gathered. The first simply is: is it more likely than not? The second is: the preponderance of the evidence.

You'll find that I can be very opinionated. So once I have completed my ranting on a subject, and you as a reader are left to ponder it, just tell me to shut up already! I will then endeavor to ask the question, "What do you think?" (This effectively takes me off the hook, kind of like a literary loophole, if you know what I mean.) I will, though, provide you with rational reasoning for why I perceive various aspects of the current written material on the Lewis and Clark Expedition boats to be false or misleading.

I have been urged for years to write a book. This endeavor is easier said than done! My family has had a good laugh at my grammar abilities over the years. They most usually like the content, but my spelling, syntax, and punctuation choices always fall under some heavy criticism. They just love to take aim at my spelling. I've heard, "He just throws commas in wherever he wants and then sprinkles in some periods!" They have dubbed me "The King of Run-On Sentences," and probably rightly so. OK, maybe I never really did grasp all of the principles of grammar, or all of the numerous rules of the English language, and my belief is that a dangling participle is something you should see a doctor about. But my attitude is simply this: if you can understand what I'm trying to tell you, who cares?

Since this is my first, and I'm confident my last, book, I was very apprehensive about it. To get an idea about how it might be received, I shared copies of it with a small group of individuals from different walks of life and different levels of formal education. It seemed a prudent way to get a feel for the general attitude about it. I will candidly admit that it was a surprising experiment. No two folks felt the same about it. Although they all generally felt it had merit, they all disagreed on which parts were interesting and which were not.

One individual felt that it could be three separate books. They made the comment that it jumped from *Popular Mechanics* to an instruction manual and then on to a story with passion and craziness. I would agree. Another person questioned me about just what I was going to call my wife: Cathy, Catherine, or my bride. I call her all of these things on a regular basis (and other personal names that I'll not be sharing with you). I cannot look at Cathy without remembering how she looked as she walked down that aisle, and I never want to forget it.

Another critique was about sentence structure and repeating certain subjects as well as being too honest about my feelings on things, both good and bad. Some felt that this gut honesty was too personal to share and did not enhance the story. I feel that since my life has been passionate and full of emotions, both good and bad, they needed to be shared so folks understand why I do what I do and why I feel the way I do about things. One individual said that when I talked about my challenging times, I sounded like I was whining. I went back and reread those parts, and I disagree. When I was unhappy about something, or felt that I failed at something, I am honest about both what caused it and my reaction to it. Ignoring these low points would do my life story a disservice. In addition to that, I generally learned valuable life lessons from every one of these experiences, and by passing that story along, I would hope to possibly influence readers to avoid something similar themselves. Lessons learned from your failures are the most valuable life lessons you can have. Then some people who read the book said that it sounds like I'm sitting there talking to them, and that pleases me immensely. That was the goal from the very beginning. Another comment was that some of my stories were not in good taste. My response is: it happened and it was funny, so it's in.

So what do I have here? Well, it's a little of this and a little of that. It's all true, and I would like to think and would bet that everyone who reads it will find something of value in it. I can tell you that I did pour my heart and soul into it. I felt it necessary to preserve the things I have learned, the theories I have developed, and my personal story. I have written this for that reason alone, not as a subject for literary scrutiny.

The task before me is to present you with evidence based on solid research, experimentation, and good ol' common sense. In this book I will not avoid drawing conclusions, and I will offer you my opinions. You may judge the validity of them for yourselves. I will also recount true tales of my "crazy" adventures along the Lewis and Clark Trail.

What do you say? Do you want to float down a path of exploration? Do you want to join me on my river travels? We'll visit a few "Knowledge Nooks" along the way. These Knowledge Nooks are similar to the question-and-answer part of my programs, where we discuss various details and how they relate to the subject at hand. As often as not, we find that one answer will lead to another question, which will take us down a path to who knows where, with that answer begging another question. Eventually we get back to where we started when I or someone else asks, "Now, where were we?" This book will do the same thing, so try to keep up!

**Chapter One**

# Prelude to the Fleet

In the winter of 1985, I was in my thirty-eighth year. A couple of years prior, I had dreamt up an idea for a high-adventure, weeklong program for the Boy Scouts. I Pied-Pipered most of my friends into helping out, and we offered it at Little Sioux Scout Ranch in Iowa. My close friend, Lewis Sloup, was the camp ranger at the time. Our first year doing this had been a roaring success, so I was raring to go on season two. I was at Little Sioux Scout Ranch with Lew one evening. We were just messing around in the shop at the ranch, building equipment, and making plans for that summer's event. That evening Old Sloup received a call from a friend of his in Onawa, Iowa.

The call was from the ranger at a state park close by. He wanted to know if Lew knew someone who could build him a model of the Lewis and Clark Expedition keelboat. With a twinkle in his eye, while he was looking right at me across the room, I heard him say, "Yeah, I might know a guy." Of course he asked me about it after he hung up, and I thought, "…build a model boat for my old buddy Lew…" Sure, why not?

That same week, I visited with the park's ranger quite extensively about how he was putting together a Lewis and Clark festival at his park near Onawa, Iowa. (The park is appropriately named Lewis and Clark State Park. Go figure!) He mentioned that I might have to do a little research to get the model details, as he'd prefer the model to look as authentic as possible. So Catherine and I headed for the library the next day. We ended up spending about two hundred hours over the course of the next month researching this boat before we finally felt we had enough information to build a pretty accurate model. (I might add, as of the writing of this book, research is ongoing.)

*Knowledge Nook:*
*Some of my thoughts concerning the boats*
*of the Lewis and Clark Expedition*

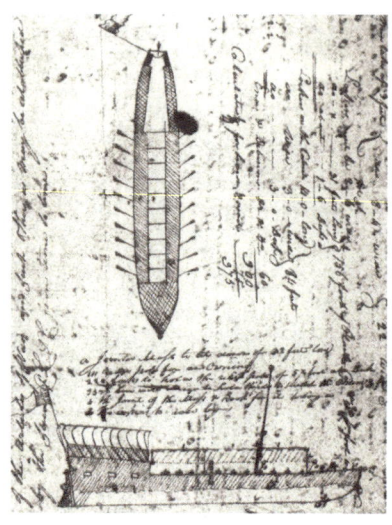

**William Clark had sketched the vessel in his field notes showing a top view and a side view.** *He never showed a bottom profile. Why didn't he feel it necessary to include the bottom design as well? He didn't have to. It was a brown-water boat. Men of that time would have just known that it would need to be flat, or nearly so, for traveling the inland waterways of the early 1800s. Some people claim this boat had a round bottom. If you agree with that, in my opinion, you're just wrong. If you know anything at all about rivercraft on any river in any country in the world, you know that they are pretty flat. They have to be. Why do you think the English so feared the Vikings?* **Their shallow-draft, nearly-flat-bottom long boats could just sail up any river in England, so they could plunder any village they wanted to.** *(If you're still thinking round bottom, that's fine; but if you're smart, you will stay in deep water and off the rivers!)*

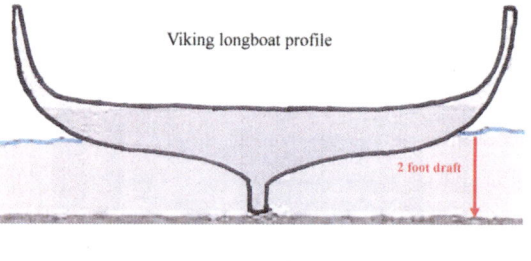

Viking longboat profile

2 foot draft

In 1993, a nautical historian, researcher, author, and avid model builder published an article in the Nautical Research Journal concerning the boats of the Lewis and Clark Expedition. I have the highest respect for his work. I do, however, respectfully disagree with some of his writings regarding the Lewis and Clark Expedition boats.

*He sees the keelboat/barge as a round-bottom craft, and I see it as a nearly flat-bottomed craft. He sees the pirogues as double-ended craft with rounded sides and a nearly flat bottom. I see them almost the same way, but*

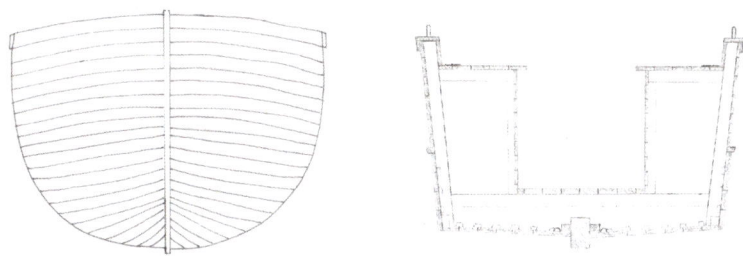

*with two differences. I see the sides as slab-like, and I believe there is ample evidence that they were pointed-bow and flat-sterned. He also states what size they were, whereas I would rather identify a possible size range that they would fall into. A small point, to be sure, but when it comes to our history, I feel you need to relay accurately whether or not you are surmising, or if you are stating fact based on evidence. The only evidence available on the pirogues at the very best gives you some idea of a size range, but not much beyond that.*

*There are some other points that we disagree on, and I will touch on them. However, I would like to point out that there are many points that we do agree on, and his article is in my library as a valuable research document. Following are my thoughts concerning our areas of disagreement.*

*The round-bottom boat would draw about three feet of water when empty. The estimate of tonnage carried on the expedition is figured to be from twelve to eighteen tons. I have tank-tested the round-bottom design, and have found that it would draw at least five feet of water with that kind of weight onboard. That would put the gunnels almost awash! (By the way, a group in Missouri built a barge using the round-bottom specifications, and it did draw approximately three feet of water with very little cargo, certainly nothing near the estimated tonnage carried.) Also, professionals and I have tested the lateral stability of the round-bottom design, and we have both found it dangerously unstable in a cordelle situation on a moving body of water without added ballast very low in the craft.*

*The Bouvier flat-bottom design draws about eighteen inches of water when empty, and with a simulated thirteen-ton cargo, it draws about two and a half feet. Thomas Rodney wrote in his journal that Lewis's barge drew two and a half feet of water when it was fully loaded. He wrote that the very evening after he visited with Lewis on his "barge"…good enough for me! That's a primary* source. The very same load and cordelle tests performed on the round-bottom design were also performed on my design. The flat-bottom model performed well, but it did have some problems when sideways to the current. For irony's sake, I'll add that you'll find in the journals that the expedition's barge experienced the same problems when sideways to the current.

## Keelboat/Barge

Not one journalist on the expedition ever referred to the large boat as a keelboat. They most often called it the Barge, the Captain's Boat, the big boat, and a couple of other names. I am confident they referred to it as a dirty, rotten s.o.b., as I have mine, many times on the river. I have no proof of that, although I would bet a good steak dinner on it! But they never called it a keelboat. While at the Wood River camp the first winter, Clark modified the barge and added what can be described as keelboat details to it. The first time I have found the word keelboat used when describing this craft was a very early document Lewis wrote describing the type of boat he would like to have for the expedition. As it turned out, he had it built in a different location by another individual, and I firmly believe that the craft built was barge-like in design.

## The Two Pirogues

I agree more than I disagree with the gentleman who published on the round-bottom design. We both feel that they were plank-built craft, i.e. flat-bottomed workboats. He shows a slightly rounded side to the craft with less of a flat bottom, and I show slab sides with more of a flat bottom. He shows only double-ended craft, and I feel there is every possibility that they were flat-sterned. I have shown both styles with my replica pirogues.

Some folks believe that the pirogues were a form of dug-out canoe. Most hinge their argument on a comment made in the journals at the Great Falls where the pirogues were laid up, as they were too large to portage to the upper falls. The comment was also made that they knocked out the "plugs of gauge" prior to covering the craft with brush and such. Let's talk a little about dugouts to help explain this term. When you make a dugout, you obviously start with a tree trunk. Some folks I have visited with say that you first roll your log into the water to see which side naturally floats up. I do know that wet wood splits out easier than dry. That could also have something to do with it. Anyway, once you decide what shape your craft will take, you do the outside first. Then you strategically drill holes in your hull and drive in plugs, which are the length of what you want for thickness in those areas. (I have never seen this in print, but

4

*I have used walnut plugs in a cottonwood hull so that the plugs would be more visible.) Now you dig out the interior of the log until you get to the plugs. This gauges your hull thickness, as a mistaken hole in the hull is disastrous. Thus the term "plugs of gauge."*

*In a plank-built boat of any size, you must have drain plugs. In modern boats they are rubber, plastic screw-in, or metal, and as often as not, they are located at the rear of the craft. On large replica wooden craft I have always put in several drain plugs, both front and rear, and often along the sides. Why? Well, when you drag them up onshore, you never really know which way the water will drain. Usually front or rear, but often you cannot control that without more effort than you or anyone else wants to put out. Also if the craft is to be stored outside during the winter, you would need as many drain holes as possible. Snow melts, refreezes into ice, and then the ice expands, exerting tremendous force, which when trapped between frames or planks on a boat can destroy the structural integrity. If the water can run out when the snow melts, it doesn't have a chance to refreeze. The more drain holes open the better!*

*I generally drill my drain holes at 3/4–1 inch, and then plug them with a hardwood plug that is slightly tapered from the hole size to slightly under. I pattern my hole size, location, and plug design after plugs I have seen in large wooden rivercraft found in the river at marine archaeological digs. These are drain plugs, but are virtually identical to "plugs of gauge" in a dugout. These guys were not professional boatbuilders, but most had knowledge of dugout construction, as they were the poor man's watercraft in the 1800s.*

*Another point about dugouts is the amount of time required to complete one. People actually think that it would take longer to hand rip the planks for the stick-built craft than to hollow out a log. They had water-powered sawmills all along the Ohio then; it wasn't the dark ages! You give me a pile of lumber, and you take a solid log, and we'll start constructing our craft. I'll have two boats of comparable size in the water before you finish digging out your first log! I have successfully completed three dugouts. Thankfully, I had the help of a Native American friend, "Chief Black and Decker of the Sears Tribe!" Let me tell you, completing three dugouts is enough for any one man's lifetime.*

*Let me make one more point about plank-built simplicity and boats that are constructed to fill an immediate need. In the late 1800s, there was a gold rush in Alaska. At one point, while following a trail that led to the gold fields, along the shores of Lake Bennett, the miners had to quickly and economically build boats to navigate the river downstream for the remaining journey to*

the gold fields. They had to rip their planks by hand, and they still built...**you guessed it—flat-bottom, slab-sided, flat-sterned boats for their one-time trip.** This was accomplished in a lushly wooded area with many trees of good "dugout" size available. You must remember that the pirogues of the Lewis and Clark Expedition, as they were most often called, were purchased as used workboats off the Ohio River. And most workboats back then were commonly made using the lowest-priced and most productive materials available. A wide-bodied, flat-bottomed, plank-built boat is quicker to build, easier to maintain, and more productive as a working craft.

My attitude concerning the "pirogues," as they were called, is that they were basic workboats from the Ohio River valley. In Rodney's journals, he describes having a boat built for his trip in this area. It was as I described, square-sterned and pointed bow, simple slab sides, and flat-bottomed. A simple craft, skiff-like in design, quick and cheap to build, and will carry a large load in shallow water. It was down-and-dirty, simple, cheap, and strong. And it sure wasn't a dugout! In all Thomas Rodney's descriptions of the types of craft being built along the shore of the Ohio River in 1804, he never once mentioned dug-outs. I have also likened them to a Mackinaw-style boat from the era. Trying to attach design names to these cottage industries of boat design and building in the early 1800s is difficult at best, and foolhardy at worst.

Here is another point on this subject: when the white pirogue almost turned over in a high wind, both Lewis and Clark said it was saved from capsizing completely by its awning and sail. I have tried putting an awning on a double-ended craft. Obviously, as the bow and stern of the craft come to a point, it leaves very little room for someone to sit, let alone an awning of any kind. Another point concerning square-sterned verses pointed-stern versions is the simple fact of what I call "footprint." The greater a boat's footprint, the shallower the draft and the more cargo it can carry. Also, a square-sterned craft is easier to build.

Another interesting thing to ponder...In 1986 Catherine and I decided to paint our first two replica pirogues. We painted the "red pirogue" red, and the "white pirogue" white. These two craft were most often referred to by their colors or color designation in the journals of the Lewis and Clark Expedition.

*Since then I've seen the pirogues commonly depicted with these colors. As far as I can establish, no one had ever described them as painted or shown them that way prior to our replicas, so Cathy and I will take the heat or the credit for that one.*

*Our reasons for painting them with the corresponding colors of their descriptive names were simple. Painting boats was common practice in the 1800s. With brown-water boats, this was not necessarily done to make the boat watertight, but rather to make the wood less pervious to water. So why worry about the wood becoming water-logged? Well, wood loses strength when soaked in water.*

*If you question that, try this experiment: take two identical yardsticks (if you can find them any more), one unpainted and one painted. Put something under each end of the yardsticks so their centers are left suspended with no support. Now find something you can rest on the center of the sticks. Try a small drinking glass; fill it with water until the sticks begin to show some bend. Note the amount of water and the bend of each yardstick. Now soak the yardsticks for an hour in your bathtub. Now repeat the test. You'll see why they sealed the wood with paint. The water-soaked, unpainted yardstick will bend readily, while the painted one will retain much of its strength. What would you prefer for your boat: weak wood or strong wood? Paint back then was linseed-oil based with turpentine as a reducer/drier with white lead or red lead as a bonding agent. So red and white would make sense, wouldn't it? However, you will not find anywhere in the journals where they ever state that these two craft were actually painted those colors.*

*I would like to tell you a true story. When I was in the army, I worked a lot in the motor pool. One day the Old Man (captain in command) brought in an air force truck. He wanted us to paint it our color, olive drab, or what you might call flat green. My buddy and I were sitting around this truck the night before she was scheduled to be painted. My buddy had a small sticker shaped like a duck. It was about half an inch tall—very small. I have no idea where he got it or why he had it, but if you knew this guy you wouldn't be surprised. Anyway, the joke of the evening was that this truck would be a "ruptured duck" among our other vehicles, as it was underpowered compared to them. So my buddy decided to stick the sticker on the driver's door, low in the corner, and we all had a good laugh. You could hardly see it because the sticker and the truck were both blue. So we all quickly forgot about this after that night. Well, you guessed it… after the truck had been painted green, one of us noticed the duck, gently peeled the sticker off, and a little blue duck appeared. It was very small, and if you were anywhere beyond ten feet away, it just looked like a smudge.*

*Over the course of the next few years, that old truck became known as the blue goose, and that is what we called her. At a reunion with my old service buddies about twenty years later, one of the guys asked me if the blue goose was still there when I shipped out, and I told him it was. His wife asked, "So the army had blue trucks also?"*

*Remember, when dealing with history, we shouldn't assume anything. Just because they were called the red and white pirogues does not mean they were painted those colors. They quite possibly were, but we don't know for sure. It could have been little more than a red or white flag as its designation. One individual claimed that one was made out of white oak and the other red oak. I say hogwash to that! I don't care what wood you have or what continent it comes from, if left unprotected it will eventually all turn the same color...gray.*

*Here is another mind teaser for you: I know for a fact that no one has shown the keelboat/barge as painted, not in pictures or in models or replicas, myself included. Clark made the comment in his field notes at Wood River that he was disappointed that Sergeant Gass could not obtain any paint to paint the newly built lockers on the barge. Question: Why would they paint the lockers if the rest of the boat was not painted?*

## Now, where were we?

After our extensive research, **I built the Lewis and Clark Expedition model, and delivered it to the park in late May of 1985.** I relayed to the park ranger that I had never built a boat the size of Lewis and Clark's craft, and it would be a hoot to try! We both toyed with the idea of having a life-sized replica of the craft at the yearly event. He said that if I could line up some committed help, he could see  about getting the lumber from the Iowa Department of Natural Resources state saw mill. I did and he did. You could definitely call that a life-changing event! I decided that just circulating in the crowd at the first Lewis and Clark Festival asking folks if they wanted to build a big (almost sixty-foot) wooden boat would probably get me marked as a nut. To avoid a bad first impression, I bummed some wood from the park's lumber scrap pile and spent a couple of days building a four-foot-long cross section of the proposed boat. **We sat the cross section in an open area and chalked out the rest of the boat on the grass.** We basically depicted a life-sized craft by roping the whole section off. I knew that would get people's attention! Then we sat the model I had built on the cross section and started Pied-Pipering again. (I think if I had been Tom Sawyer, we would have made a full-time business out of painting fences.)

During that first festival, we signed up over thirty people who wanted to help on the project and make it a reality. By that fall we had a group formed (which would become "The Friends of Discovery") and had already built a strongback on which to construct the hull. We were on our way! **By the next festi-**

**val, in June of 1985, we had a watertight hull completed, so we launched her in Blue Lake and had a ball pushing her around.** A few days later, after we had launched the empty hull, we were busy tying it up at the shoreline. A little girl, maybe ten years old, was standing on the shoreline watching us. As we hopped ashore she asked, "Hey, Mister, can I get on it?" Heck, why not? So we put her aboard and showed her around. Once back onshore, as she was walking away, I heard her say, "That was neat!" I didn't realize it at that moment, but she had planted a seed in me that would grow over the years to come.

**At the next festival in 1987, our replica was complete, with a cabin, mast, and oars, and floating proudly on Blue Lake at Lewis and Clark State Park.** Mission accomplished! Catherine and I decided to name her *Discovery*, in honor of the Corps of Discovery of the Expedition, and we christened her as such.

Interesting side note: When I proudly stuck the name *Discovery* on our new creation, one of the park officials said that he did not think it was a good idea, as it could mislead people. It seemed simple enough. We named our replica, even though the original was never referred to with a name. People should understand a simple concept like that, right? It seemed right until about 2004, when the US Postal Service released a special set of Lewis and Clark Expedition commemorative stamps. I hurried to get a set, and the written documents furnished with the stamps explained how the expedition went up the Missouri in a fifty-five-foot keelboat named *Discovery*! OK, so I was wrong on this one. My kids would want to put it on the calendar just to get my goat. They have had this little saying, which they have proudly put on T-shirts and other stuff for me, "Woodwright, Boatwright, Always Wright." Not this time. I guess it's nice that something Cathy and I did actually influenced the US government, but I would have been much happier if it had been accurate!

Soon after, most of the volunteers drifted away from the project, but by then I was hooked! **So I started building the white pirogue, which was launched the very next year.** And I just kept on going.

**The red pirogue was launched in 1989.** We now had replicated the entire fleet of the Lewis and Clark Expedition! For the next six years, we gained loads of experience on how to best operate these craft on Blue Lake. We gave many folks the opportunity to ride aboard and experience it for themselves.

Around 1995 I became overwhelmed with work of all sorts, and I myself drifted away from the park and the boats. Tensions were high, and the group and I disagreed on just about everything. Frustrated, I just stepped away. I have learned some valuable life lessons over the years, and this was one: Just because you are passionate about something, you cannot just assume others will share that passion. I also need to remember that self-confidence can be easily mistaken for arrogance.

So 1999 rolled around, and there had not been anyone with the passion, skills, or confidence necessary to maintain these boats for almost five years. **The beautiful boats sat ashore and rotted to a point where they were useless and heading for the boneyard.** Then

Catherine and I went to the Iowa State Fair that year and found ourselves in the Department of Natural Resources building. As luck would have it, I spotted the director of state parks, so *carpe diem* was on the agenda.

We had a nice talk, and I pointed out that with the bicentennial of the Lewis and Clark Expedition fast approaching, it would be quite embarrassing for the State of Iowa to have nothing but rotted hulls to show to the public. He seemed to agree, as he requested that I do a complete survey of all three craft and report back to him with my proposal for repairing them, both physically and aesthetically. Within a month, I had a bound, eighty-page proposal. In fact, I made about twenty copies and mailed them off to the head of the Department of Natural Resources. Well, I guess not all of them…one or two got sidetracked and ended up with our governor and his lieutenant. You see, I didn't care to trust *any* politically driven public servant based just on a private conversation that had taken place, unless it were to be backed up in writing. And I had nothing in writing.

Well, I guess someone agreed with my proposition. Within six months, L&C Replicas was under contract to completely rebuild all three craft. The project was billed as a restoration, and it was for the pirogues. But the keelboat/barge was older than both of them, and had suffered the hand of neglect much worse. As it ended up, **we had to completely rebuild her, utilizing only about thirteen percent of the original components.** When the new *Discovery* was launched in the summer of 2000, she should have been christened *Discovery II,* according to naval guidelines concerning restorations of boats. **But nonetheless, she and her fleet were whole again.**

I have been asked a thousand times why I love building wooden boats, and I don't really know how to answer that. I can tell you this: once you take a pile of wood and form it into a beautiful boat, and then put it in water and have it take you where you want to go, you are hooked. You're asking a static product (wood) to perform a dynamic function (your boat) and have successfully coaxed all those straight boards into graceful curves that will creak and talk to you in a gentle swell. Well, enough said; it's pretty cool!

I am now also recognized as the official historian at Lewis and Clark State Park, and have continued to maintain the floating and fully operational boats for use as historical educational tools at the park. You noticed that I used the term *educational* in that last sentence. That term eluded me for many years, but another one of my crazy adventures in 2001 changed all that and made me realize that the seed planted by that little ten-year-old girl back in 1985 had sprouted and grown.

# Chapter Two

# Dawn of an Adventure

## June 2001

Catherine and I were headed to Vermillion, South Dakota, on an evening business excursion. I was to address the city fathers of the community on a proposed Lewis and Clark fishing pier, which was to look somewhat like an expedition keelboat. Along with us was Mike Butler, who was to assist with a portion of the presentation, and his wife, Lora. A local lawyer by the name of Casey had asked me to present the proposed design that evening in hopes of raising enough interest and funds for the pier. He was a wheelchair-bound young man who was very persuasive, and I had liked him right away. The project itself never did get off the drawing board, but our drive up and back that evening gave birth to quite an adventure!

You see, I-29 between Onawa, Iowa, and Vermillion, South Dakota, is within sight of the Missouri River more often than it is not. On the drive up, we found ourselves conversing about how the river above Sioux City was pretty much in its original state, not having been modified to any great extent by the Corps of Engineers. Despite a few dams, we were driving right next to that long stretch of untouched river, very much like what Lewis and Clark would have seen in 1804. I couldn't help but think about how it would feel to navigate the Missouri in a boat similar to the type of workboat that plied our inland waterways in the eighteenth and nineteenth centuries. At this time, I had been designing and building these replica craft for almost thirteen years. Having run them on Blue Lake and worked out many of the problems of how to make them do what they needed to do on a stationary body of water, I couldn't help but think it was time to take the next step and get out on a river. I shared the notion that I'd love to run that stretch of river in a replica Mackinaw. Mike eagerly agreed that such an expedition could be one heck of an adventure! We chitchatted on the topic the entire rest of the drive up.

During the presentation that evening, my mind kept revisiting the conversation in the car. When I turned the presentation over to Mike for a short time, my mind was drawn back to thoughts about making that trip! Somehow we got through the presentation (which was very good, even with me daydreaming through it). After the presentation, we visited and enjoyed conversation with other Lewis and Clark buffs in the audience. I shared my newfound enthusiasm for journeying that stretch of the river. One guy told us that he had canoed that same stretch of river several times.

He stated that nothing larger than a johnboat could get through it because it was too shallow. That had my curiosity piqued! I asked him just how shallow it was. He said that in some places it was only one foot deep, but averaged about two feet. His view was that, two hundred years ago, that stretch of river must have been much deeper.

Well, we know that the Lewis and Clark keelboat/barge itself drew about two and a half feet loaded to the gills. She scraped bottom many times, and if she strayed from any of the deeper sections of the river at all, she had trouble. I believe the main channel in 1804 averaged about five feet. Even at that, a five-foot-deep channel does not allow too much room for error. Which is exactly why when she reached the Mandan Villages in North Dakota, it was determined that she could no longer continue. The pirogues of the expedition, which I believe were Mackinaw-styled craft, on the other hand, probably drew no more than eighteen inches, and could therefore continue. And they did, all the way to the Great Falls. Had they not been too large to portage, they could have gone even further.

I don't recall much else from that conversation. I had been calculating. At this time, with quite a few years of studying and building nineteenth-century rivercraft under my belt, I knew their draft was far less than two and one half feet when empty, and with proper design, could be less than two feet, maybe as little as eighteen inches. After visiting for quite some time, the four of us decided to head for home. We said our good-byes, and as we were loading into the vehicle, my mind was still playing with ideas for designs of a craft that could navigate such a shallow passage. On the drive back, I told Mike that I was certain that I could design a boat to travel that shallow stretch of river—and with several tons of supplies onboard! That sure drew his interest. We all talked excitedly about the idea of making that voyage. We stopped in Sioux City at a truck stop for some pie and coffee. The conversation about the boat continued as **I bummed a paper towel from the waitress and sketched out my design (I still have that paper towel).** We all agreed that she would be a great boat to build. By the time we reached home, I had planned to do just that…some day.

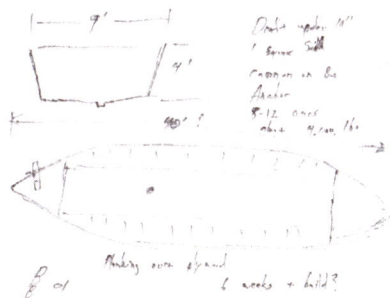

My wife just recently confided to me that before we returned to Onawa that evening she knew that I would be building that boat! (I think sometimes she knows me better than I know myself.) I did have the final design complete within the next week. And yes, I was quite eager to build that boat and plan an expedition! But could I just put everything on hold to build it and journey up the river? Well, how could we fail?…With her support, my set of skills, and money enough to buy materials? OK, so I didn't have the money, but that's the story of my life! We were going to build it, and that was that!

*Knowledge Nook:*
*More on pre-steam era boatbuilding and design*

*Most blue-water boatbuilders just don't understand riverboat building of the nineteenth century. This became very evident when the Smithsonian hired a nautical engineer to draw up plans for the expedition keelboat based on Clark's drawings in his field notes from his time at Wood River in the winter of 1804–*

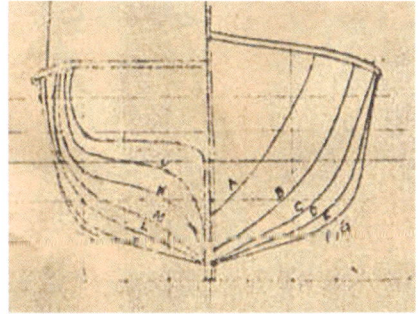

*1805. The engineer had it right until he did the hull cross section. **He designed a beautifully contoured and rounded hull, which would sail well in ocean swells, and would probably draw only three feet of water when empty (if it could even float on an even keel without ballast).** But after calculating in the cargo it would have had onboard, the boat he designed would not have floated in the Missouri River of 1804. That makes two very knowledgeable and better-educated-than-me individuals who feel that this craft was round-bottomed. Both of these gentlemen are no*

doubt experts when it comes to salt-water ocean-going craft. But brown-water boats are a horse of a different color.

Very early in my boatbuilding career, I found myself fascinated with pre-steam era rivercraft of all kinds. My interest was piqued because there were very few written documents on the subject, and even fewer plans or drawings. After twenty years of trial and error and thousands of hours of researching through documents, paintings, drawings, experiments, and whatever else was available, I have come to the following conclusions about seventeenth–nineteenth-century American rivercraft. They were all built with a shallow draft, and they were designed for flexibility along the length.

Now, ocean-going craft needed a deep draft for stability in high seas, and for good sailing characteristics. The vessel had to be stiff and inflexible to take the pounding of the heavy seas and large swells. Rivercraft, on the other hand, did not require great sailing ability, as it was not their primary method of propulsion. If the craft were constructed too rigid and got stuck on a sandbar, it would break its back without some flexibility built in. And often, they still broke even if they were flexible!

When the great steamboats came along in the mid-1800s, many of them had one similar unique feature, which actually indicates just how important brown-water boat flexibility was to their survival. **This feature was called a hogging chain.** It was literally a huge chain, or more often linked bars, which ran from the keel in the bow to the keel in the stern. Usually it was two chains: one on each side of the boat. They ran up and 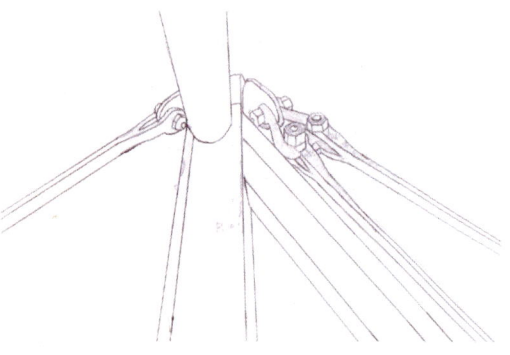 through (or over) the main structure and had a huge turnbuckle near their center. By tightening or loosening these chains, they could actually change the shape of the hull on the boat. This could be used to stiffen it for large deck cargo or to make it more flexible to get off a sandbar. Try that with a blue-water boat!

Concerning inland watercraft prior to the twentieth century, all rivercraft and lakecraft around the world shared some common traits. In addition to their shallow-draft capability, they had a simplistic design and were constructed of many woods that were not generally used in building blue-water boats. As often as not, they were built quickly and from necessity, using whatever materials were available. Generally speaking, if they were constructed at a boatbuilding area where there were sawmills set up, builders would use lumber from the surrounding forests. There were no semitrucks or railroads to transport special lumber in from far away. If wood had to be brought in from elsewhere, it was generally from somewhere upstream. It may have been brought in by another brown-water boat, or it may have just been sent floating down the stream as a raft chained together.

Now, in the wilderness, where boats were constructed when a need presented itself, such as to get a person and his possessions back downstream, boatbuilders would have just cleared an area at the water's edge. The trees they had cleared would have been used as the building material. I'd say, the bigger the clearing one came across, the bigger the boat that had been constructed there. And why at the water's edge, you ask? Well, the boats were heavy, and they would have needed to be taken to the water's edge when completed.

This is also a good time to talk about the types of wood used in boatbuilding throughout the ages. Generally speaking, if you had been building a blue-water boat, your choice of woods would have been somewhat limited. You would have been looking for strength, availability, and rot resistance, as these crafts' upkeep were a huge investment in time and resources, and the craft constructed with them were expected to last twenty years or more. White oak, spruce, yellow pine, and exotics (like mahogany and teak) were sought after and used when available. Common pine, cottonwood, walnut, and other widespread fast-growing trees usually would not have been considered for one of these craft. Plain and simple, blue-water boatbuilders needed to be particular about the material they used.

Brown-water boatbuilders did not worry about wood rotting over time because usually their boats would not have survived too long on the snag-infested rivers prior to 1900. Often, they were used once and then abandoned. I have heard many times that once abandoned, they were sold as scrap lumber for building homes nearby. I do not believe that these purpose-built Mackinaw and keelboat-style craft befell this early form of recycling. When it comes to boats with a pointed bow and plank built over frames, there is just not much usable lumber of any decent size on them. And more often than not, getting them apart would be more trouble than just hand milling lumber from a tree. Many of these purpose-built, one-trip boats were from planks split with wedges rather than sawn with a pit saw. This early recycling may have been the case with large, **flat boats (or Longhorns as they were called), as they were heavily planked, pretty large, and rectangular in shape.** Longhorns were designed to float downstream only. They were guided by river currents, sweeps or steering oars, and set poles. Once they reached their destina-  tion, they became a prime source of lumber, since they contained large pieces, and the pieces were pretty straight and had a limited number of fasteners.

No matter the type of boat being built, when selecting wood from the locally available lumber, whether in the city with mills, or in the wilderness along the rugged river, all builders, if prudent, would look over the lumber before deciding how each piece would be used. For instance, if you had an oak tree and a cottonwood tree to choose from, the appropriate decision would be to choose the oak for the keel and frames, and the cottonwood for the planking. Oak is strong and would hold fasteners, whether wood or metal, and cottonwood can easily be bent when green.

Use what you have at hand, but use it judiciously. Often, when I am giving a program, I tell the audience that there was only one kind of wood used when constructing brown-water boats before 1900; it was the one closest to the building site! I do feel fairly comfortable stating that there has been a boat, or a part of a boat, built from just about every type of tree known to man!

My choice of construction techniques and woods for replicas falls into two categories. If I am building a historically accurate exact replica, I want to use the plank-on-frame method, which was common prior to 1900. I would pick and choose wood from local sources. Now if I'm constructing a replica for resilience, I figured out that if I first built the boat from plywood and then over-planked it with thinner planking, it would be strong and look authentic. It would also be very near the same hull thickness and weight of the authentic craft, and thus would act the same in the water. Now this type of authentic-looking and authentic-acting craft would still rot unless I could find a way to stop that process. The old-timers who built these craft to use back in the day did not concern themselves with rot, as longevity was really not an issue for them. It was a definite concern for me, as I did not want to pour my blood, sweat, and tears into something that would begin to rot before I even got it launched!

*My first thought was pressure-treated plywood. Every lumberyard I talked to and the wooden-boat society in general said the same thing. Pressure-treated plywood was not of high-enough quality, it would not hold fasteners well, and the glue was not waterproof and would fail with constant exposure to water.*

*Treated lumber is of a lower quality than quarter-sawn tight-grained traditional boat lumber, but using larger pieces overcomes that problem. So the next question is: won't that make the boat heavier? The answer is: not enough to be a problem! When you're comparing tight-grained hard wood to a softer wood of the same size, the hard wood will be heavier. Double the size of the soft wood to get the same strength, and the difference in weight between the two is not as great as one may think.*

*That dilemma aside, now how does one get fasteners to hold well? Using larger fasteners and more of them takes care of this. Gluing, or beading as we call it, all the joints and precisely cutting and fitting them so the fasteners cannot shift at all keeps everything nice and tight. Still, it would not do well to have your boat delaminate and sink! The problem of the non-waterproof glue failing under constant exposure to water seemed unsolvable until the fall of 2000...*

*My longtime friend, Russ Field, was the Department of Natural Resources technician at Lewis and Clark State Park from 1983 to 2005. Every autumn he pulled all the docks in from the lake for the winter. I offered my assistance for this task in the fall of 2000. We were to dismantle one to salvage the flotation units, as it would be replaced with a new one the next spring. I helped him turn it over to access the flotation devices, which were boxed with plywood. The fasteners around the edges were welded in place with rust, so we dropped a skill saw in and cut out the center. It was treated plywood! This treated plywood had been fully immersed for ten seasons and was still in perfect shape! Plywood does not delaminate in water! I was to follow the convention of my predecessors and use locally available materials. (But mine would not rot!)*

## Now, where were we?

I began lofting and building frames for the replica white pirogue in late July of 2000, and I spent just about every weekend on it until it was launched the week before our adventure in October. Now as I said, I have surmised that the pirogues of the Lewis and Clark Expedition were built-up, plank-on-frame craft, similar to Mackinaw boats that worked on our inland waterways around that time. Ours was to be forty-two feet long with a beam at the waterline of eight feet—a nearly flat-bottomed craft with very little dead rise.

Her draft was designed to be no more than twelve inches from the bottom of the keel. She would have a twenty-foot mast and carry two hundred square feet of main sail and eight square feet of spritsail. She would have walkways along her length and six sets of thole pins on each side, which would accommodate twelve oars, each thirteen feet long. A sweep (rudder) of laminated ash would give her good control. The twelve thirteen-foot oars would be complimented by as many set poles, and a cannon on the bow would repel river pirates, and would let everyone know when we were coming. OK, probably no river pirates, but we sure did have fun with it!

I spent many hours researching and planning for this trip. I drove the route and made contacts, and I gathered and purchased materials we would need. In all, I spent about four months preparing for this adventure. All the while, I worked feverishly to complete the boat so we could actually make the trip a reality! I invited the volunteer group, Friends of Discovery, to co-sponsor this expedition. This would help showcase our fundraising efforts for a new visitor's center at Lewis and Clark State Park, which the Friends group was heading up. This group was based at the state park and sponsored by the Iowa Department of Natural Resources.

I struck a deal with the Friends group; Catherine and I would organize and plan the project, design the boat, and cover any expenses that were not covered by donations for the trip. The Friends group members would put as much time as they could on the boat, and design and build the trailer under the guidance of Mike Butler. Their "sweat equity" would earn them a spot on the trip.

Cathy and I funded the entire project out of our pockets and beat the bushes for donations to help out. Our reasons were honest and straightforward. We wanted to promote the new visitor center, the park, and our new company, L&C Replicas. We offered everyone who helped on the project a free ride and a spot on the boat. Besides the cost of building the boat, we also took care of most of the motel rooms when needed, and all of the food for the group. Some questioned our intentions, but Cathy and I didn't let that slow us down, as we felt that the ultimate outcome would show that our plans were honorable and in the best interests of everyone.

We planned for the Friends group members to act as boat and ground crew. This quickly expanded as word of our plans leaked out to the Lewis and Clark community. A dentist in Frankfort, Kentucky, Dr. Rod, quickly known to us as "Doc," and his son Nate heard of our plans via the Internet. They contacted me, wanting a spot on the crew. I was intrigued by their interest, so I told them when and where to show up, and I would sign them up as crewmembers. They showed up, and I signed them up. I met Dale at the Lewis and Clark Festival in June. He was an educator and reenactor, so we had a lot of common interests. We struck up a friendship, and I invited him to join us. I didn't find out until later that he really never thought I would pull it off. Dale turned out to be a valuable member of our little expedition; we were very fortunate to have him along.

Bill was in management for a large company with an interest in the future of the Missouri River. He heard about what we were doing and offered a substantial donation for a seat on the boat. Tim is the CEO of another major company in Sioux City. He was Gary's employer at the time; Gary was a new member of the Friends group. Tim also wanted to go along, and he offered a cash incentive for his seat. I took him up on his offer with a little apprehension, but the cost of this adventure was beginning to spin out of control, and we needed investors. Knowing what I know now, I would have paid him to join us. He is an exceptional individual, and it was an honor to have him along!

Mike Butler introduced me to Frank and Vicki Koeppe in July of 2000. Mike had suggested that Frank and his truck would be an excellent choice to haul the *Raycliff* to Fort Randall Dam for our trip that fall. Little did I know that it would kick off a long-term friendship. Frank had not planned to join us on the trip, as he and water did not get along. But once we got to Fort Randall, he and Vicki just got caught up in the thing, and he jumped onboard for the adventure of a lifetime!

Then a state senator, Steve, and I had met during the rebuild of *Discovery* in the early spring of 2000. At the time there was some controversy about the Missouri River, and he wanted to see firsthand what was going on. I invited him along, and he hooked up with us at about the halfway point, and we enjoyed his company immensely. We have all heard the stories about powerful and important men being "down to earth" individuals. All I can tell you is this: when he crawled out of his pup tent in the morning and wandered over to where Dale and I had the coffee pot on with an empty cup in his hand, he was definitely an equal, as everyone else was doing the same thing! A neat guy, Cathy and I grew to like and respect him very much. Cathy and I were among some of the first folks to know of his intended run for US Congress, as he gave us both a T-shirt announcing it. We still have the shirts and cherish them. Along the way, we picked up some other individuals for a day or partial day on the river. We had one heck of a crew!

**Onboard crew:** Dale, Bill, Tim, Gary, Hans, Mike Butler, Wayne, Nathan Butler, Frank Koeppe, Larry McElroy, Willy Dahl, Robbie, Terry, Dr. Rod "Doc," Nate

**Part-time crew:** Cathy Bouvier, Senator Steve, Vicky Koeppe

**Ground crew:** Butch Bouvier, Catherine Bouvier, Lora Butler, Karolyn McElroy, Becky, Deanna, Leonard, Vicki Koeppe, Elaine

One of my brainstorms was to provide everyone with a blank, leather-bound journal and a quill pen and ink, and charge each of them to keep a personal journal of the adventure. Out of twenty journals handed out, only four members of the crew completed one and returned it to me. I told each journalist that some day I hoped to publish them. Cathy and I had planned ahead of time to just keep notes and photos and write ours as a commentary on all the others.

When editing these journals, I decided to lump all journal entries and my commentary together by day. I used this same procedure when researching the Lewis and Clark Expedition from the three "bibles." Dr. Gary Moulton, who edited the journals of the expedition, Donald Jackson, who edited the letters of the expedition, and Smith and Wick, who edited Thomas Rodney's journals—each editor presented the journals or letters using different outlines, but none of them used my outline. When I first started my research back in the mid-1980s, I kept getting lost looking for references to the boats of the expedition. Finally I decided to take every reference to the boats from each of the three sources and put them in chronological order. This allowed me to see at a glance what everyone was saying about what happened that day, and then I could compare the comments to better understand what was going on. This endeavor took about four months and yielded a two-hundred-page document, which then became my primary resource over the proceeding years. The following journals are also chronological by day. You'll be able to read what everyone said about each particular day. This will help give you a complete picture of what was happening on that day, and it may make you wonder if we were all on the same trip! Just as the journals of Lewis and Clark were, the journals of the Triumphant Return of the White Pirogue would be no different.

Since my perspective of this adventure is an overall view, with a lot of behind-the-scenes info no one else had, I will comment as needed to clarify and enhance your understanding of the day-to-day activities of my group on this week-long experience. My commentary after each crewmember's daily entry shows my mind-set from within a few weeks of the journey and now some twelve years later. Some may not like the repetition of the "Triumphant

Return journals," but if you read them carefully, you will find funny little details that differ from one journalist to another, and these differences will enhance your understanding of the events. Also, these journals are presented as written, except for names left out or changed to protect identities.

# *Building Raycliff*

I had sketched a rough design on a napkin the night we came back from our flopped presentation that gave this adventure its birth. A week later, I had worked out some more details, and we actually began building within about two weeks.

We decided to name her the *Raycliff.* Mike's wife came up with this, as he and I had dreamed up this crazy idea. His middle name is Raymond, and mine is Clifton.

**First we built the frames and keel and attached them to each other in the building shed.** We hurriedly sheeted and planked her bottom, down to about the waterline. I say *down,* as we built her inverted to facilitate construction.

**We spent some time bracing her internally,** as she was nothing more than a bottom and some exposed frames at this point. Next we had to turn her over. **This was a bit tricky, as we had little room to work. But with some homemade A-frames and come-a-longs, we slowly got her halfway over.** Next we had to re-rig the chains and such to let her down without hurting either her or the crew. **Finally, late that night, she was over and sitting on her own keel.** We all wanted to celebrate, but were just too tired, so we just killed all the lights and went home.

That next day, we started to build up her sides and stiffen her interior. *Raycliff* was first sheeted with 3/4-inch treated plywood: two layers on the bottom and up to the waterline, and then one sheet from there up. Once that was done, **I over-planked her with 1 and 1/4 inch (we call it 5/4-inch) round-nose treated lumber.** I edge-glued all of that for extra strength, and then screwed everything together.

Once all that was done, it was time to get busy with the five-quarter-inch cedar for all the interior and upper works.

It was exciting building the interior out of cedar. You could tell that she was going to be a beautiful boat once all was painted or varnished. We continued the exterior planking process, but it was slowed down a bit because I had designed a double-ended craft, which required bending and fitting just about every other plank. In our hurry to get her turned over, **I had overlooked the painting of the bottom, so everyone pitched in to help as we tilted her to paint first one side then the other.**

At last we had the exterior built and could concentrate on the interior. I knew that she would have to be very strong on deck, as she would not be handled with kid gloves on the river. I also made the decision that we would stain the cedar to help it maintain its color and give it a richer tone.

**Once again the ladies pitched in to help with this.** I do believe that they enjoyed this more than reaching under her and painting above their heads. Jokingly, they said that it was a wonder that I hadn't turned her over to stain the interior.

She was finally done, and so was her trailer. Mike brought it over, and we wasted no time getting her loaded. **We congratulated each other on a job done quickly but well, and got ready to get her wet for the first time.** We christened her *Raycliff* and backed her down the boat ramp to her new environment. **Cathy got a chance to get in on the launching, as she had only been able to help with the build on weekends.**

*Raycliff* floated wonderfully, and without any leaks at all! **We decided to play with her a bit on the lake just to see how she handled.** She was all lady, and could turn on a dime and glide along for eighty feet or more with one push-off. We had a winner, and we couldn't wait to test her on the Missouri River. Done at last, and the adventure could begin!

The day we launched her, I discovered that my estimate of twelve inches of draft was off. This seven-thousand-pound craft drew less than ten inches of water. No computers with auto-cad programs, just historic designs, which had also been figured out by our predecessors two hundred years ago. We were ready to go!

The Lewis and Clark Expedition keelboat was sent back from the Mandan winter camp under the control of Cpl. Richard Worfington in the spring of 1805. It carried some guys who were no longer needed, and most of the journals and items collected up to that point. However, the little white pirogue was the only original expedition craft to be used on the return trip by Lewis and Clark, and I have always referred to it as "The Triumphant Return of the White Pirogue."

## Chapter Three

# Journals of The Triumphant Return of the White Pirogue

*Daily entries by: Dale, Bill, Tim, Gary, and Butch Bouvier*

## Dale
### June 9–10, 2001

I was at a Lewis and Clark event in Onawa, Iowa (the seventeenth annual Lewis and Clark Festival at the state park), where I met a strange man by the name of Butch Bouvier. Butch is a boatwright in Onawa. Who in the devil would build wooden boats in Iowa? Butch! He looked at my display of Patrick Gass tools and said he believed that I should have some caulking tools. He told me he would send me some pictures of the tools; he would even send me an original caulking tool he had so that I might have Randy reproduce one for me—yeah, sure!

### June 28, 2001

Butch called me tonight and said he planned on sending me the tool. Yeah, sure—but he wanted to talk about a boat trip he had planned for the first week in October 2001. Great idea, but he hadn't started building the pirogue yet. I have heard some real BS in my life, but this man is a professional. He asked me to come along and work with the young people who he was inviting come to the river and look at the pirogue (that wasn't yet built). I said yes on the spot, but I knew it would not happen by October 2001. There were too many loose ends to put together.

### July 12, 2001

Butch called and asked me to come to Council Bluffs to meet with some other people who are going to raise money for the trip that is now known as The Triumphant Return of the White Pirogue—but no pirogue yet.

### July 24, 2001

Joan and I drove to Council Bluffs, and sure enough, there were people there—Gary, and some educators from Iowa. They all seemed to be normal people, even Butch's wife, Catherine. They were all fired up. I still think Butch is full of BS. There isn't enough time to pull this off.

### August 17, 2001

Lonnie and I stopped in Onawa on our way to Sioux City to look at the white pirogue. It is started, but I am right; there isn't enough time to get it done by October 1, 2001. Butch is smoking dope in his pipe.

### September 21, 2001

I got a letter from Butch with pictures of the finished pirogue, plus maps, a crew roster, etc. I am eating crow pie as I pack my bags for an adventure of a lifetime.

### September 28, 2001

I taught all day at the museum and got home at about 4:00 p.m. to finish packing the things I forgot—a Hudson Bay start, just like Lewis and Clark. I bid AJ, my old and faithful friend and traveling mate for the last fourteen-plus years, his last earthly farewell. Old age had caught up to him. I hope he understood what I tried to tell him—I think he did. I left town feeling less of a man for making Joan and Lonnie do a job I couldn't bring myself to do.

My mileage was 67,400 when I headed the truck east and north for the big Missouri. It was about 9:30 when I checked into the Onawa Super 8 for my last bed and shower for a few days or maybe a week. Went to the local watering hole to meet Butch and some of the crew. Dr. Rod Whitaker and his son Nate were still there with Butch. It was late, and we all took off for bed. We are going to start loading the pirogue at 8:00 a.m. Butch has it finished!

# Day One: The Trip Begins

## Dale
### Saturday, September 29, 2001

I am just like a little kid on his way to scout camp for the first time—awake at 4:00 a.m., checking the clock to make sure I didn't oversleep and miss the boat—no, it is a white pirogue. We checked out of the motel at 7:00 a.m. and grabbed breakfast at Big Mac's. After we started for the lake, I remembered that I left my medicine bag on the bathroom door when I showered. Bad medicine—turned around in the middle of the trail and went back to get it. I was the first one at the lake, so I drove around the campground. When I got back, the crew had started to gather. Met Frank the truck driver for the first time. There was something about Frank that I liked—maybe it was because my dad was a truck driver. I don't know.

We loaded the pirogue with very little trouble. We had more trouble getting everyone's cargo loaded. It looked like we were all going away to college. Terry, the photographer from Lyons, Nebraska, had a small trailer at his house, so he and I drove over and got it. We were now behind schedule. It was 11:00 a.m. before we hit the road. It looked like a caravan out of *The Grapes of Wrath*: pickups with stuff on top, trailers wrapped in canvas, but no pregnant women or dirty children. Stopped in Ponca, Nebraska, for lunch at the city park, and the local folk came out to take pictures. We got to Lake Francis Case at Fort Randall Dam at about 5:00 p.m. We put the pirogue in the water and ate at about 9:00 p.m. and went to bed. A good day, with good weather. The adventure has begun, and I am dead tired.

## Butch Bouvier
### October 2001

When I first dreamed this thing up, I immediately thought of Dale. I was very impressed with him when we met in June. I read him as a "can-do" guy, and I tend to gravitate toward those kinds of folks. Life is too short to talk things to death, so I surround myself with people who want to get things done: people who are skilled, intelligent, and kind. And I insist on high moral character and a good attitude. Some may think me arrogant or too picky, but my daddy told me that if I hung out with dogs I'd catch fleas.

This thing we call life is *not* a dress rehearsal; it's the real deal. And we need to treat it as such and do it right the first time!

I did send Dale the caulking iron, and he did have his friend reproduce two copies of it, as I had mentioned that I had wished I had two. We now both have what we want.

Dale's instincts about Frank Koeppe were right on. Frank is a grand guy, and I believe he has skills that he has never tapped. Dale and I have made it a goal of ours to help him develop them.

Getting packed and on the road that first day resembled refugees fleeing an advancing army. In order to convince the non-campers among the group, I had said they could bring along as much stuff as they wanted, as we would have ample ground vehicles to haul it. OK, so that was a stupid thing to say… too late now. I looked really hard, and I did not find a kitchen sink, but I was convinced it would show up eventually. Once we were finally on the road, things smoothed out, and we were all very anxious to get to Fort Randall Dam. Dale had it right; it felt just like going to summer camp.

There were many amateur campers along, and I had to assume responsibility immediately to ensure that the ground crew successfully fulfilled its mission. As it turned out, my responsibilities to the ground crew kept me from spending even one day on the river with my beautiful new boat. A terrible personal disappointment, but I never let on to anyone that it was anything other than what I had planned and wanted. Keeping the folks excited and happy was key to the success of this adventure, and that was what I wanted—total success. You can set the tone for the group with your attitude if you're the leader, so I kept it positive at all times, even when I could hardly stand to see my creation cast off and leave the dock each day without me.

That first full day at Fort Randall was interesting, to say the least. My challenge was to pull the group together. Although I felt that I had made strides in that direction by the end of the day, I still was very concerned about the conduct of a few. I resolved myself to watch this situation very carefully, as it could be our undoing if I did not get a handle on it.

## Butch Bouvier
### *2013*

I have read Dale's first entries many times, and I always get a chuckle out of them. He is a well-educated man with a good sense of humor, which I have always appreciated. He tells it the way he sees it. I have not seen Dale for about five years, but I would bet that he hasn't changed a lick! Frank Koeppe and his wife Vicky remain good friends who I see often, as they live nearby. Frank really came out of his shell on this trip and the ones to follow, but that's yet to come. With Dale and me helping him, he went from caterpillar to butterfly aboard the *Raycliff*.

The day we left for this adventure, I knew I would have some logistical challenges ahead of me, but the personality conflicts almost overwhelmed me. Looking back on it, I now realize that I had set too high a standard for everyone. I knew what I expected of myself in this endeavor, and I just assumed that everyone else felt the same way. My enthusiasm for some of the crazy stuff I do is infectious, but I realize now that to automatically assume that everyone shared my level of excitement was foolhardy.

## Gary
### *Saturday, September 29, 2001*

The day started with a wonderful sunrise. A mist rose gently from Blue Lake, and Canadian geese were just starting to go out to feed. Mike and Nathan were working on the boat, and we all were anticipating the arrival of the truck and driver.

Mike, Nathan, Hans, and I rowed the boat to the north dock, and the trailer was backed into the lake. The loading went well. Departure time was to be 10:00 a.m. but did not occur until after noon. I ran our dog, Bruno, to the vet in Mapleton and came back to finish packing the car. We loaded food, clothing, and gear for three people for a week into a small Chevy. I don't know how we did it, but it got done. There was no room for anything more, so we had to wear part of our costumes to save space.

It took until 5:30 p.m. to reach Fort Randall Dam, where we pitched camp and feasted on pork loins and baked potatoes. Our tent was borrowed from Buffalo Bill Sanders and proved to be versatile and easy to use.

## Butch Bouvier
### *October 2001*

We had high hopes that Gary's dog could go with us, but a week prior to the event, we discovered the animal was seriously ill. That was a disappointment for us, and I believe heartbreaking for Gary. Gary and his wife are pretty new to our group, and they're well on their way to being some of our most valued members.

## Butch Bouvier
### *2013*

Looking back, two of our key people were brokenhearted over their four-legged sidekicks, which spoke volumes about their character and endeared them both even more to me.

A couple of years after the trip, Gary took another job and left our community. I have most often worked with the Lewis and Clark State Park Friends group during my adventures. This hard-working group of folks is like a family; and like many families, they argue about almost everything. This internal discontent has as often as not caused them to fall short of their goals and lead those outside the group to be suspicious of their motives. I have heard it said that if you lay a wooden spoon over a boiling pot of potatoes, it would not boil over. Individuals with Gary's level of professionalism were the wooden spoons the group needed.

## Tim
### *Comments*

It all started when Gary told me about the planned voyage of the white pirogue. At first I just wanted to be a part of the community project. As I thought about it, I knew I wanted to take this once-in-a-lifetime opportunity to follow the path of Lewis and Clark.

## Tim
### *Saturday, September 29, 2001*

When my brother Dick and I reached Fort Randall Dam early on Saturday afternoon, we discovered that we were the first to arrive. We scouted out the park to see what was there, and we were ready when the party arrived. The boat was beautiful! So shapely and lovely, with dark, varnished trim. **She was also fresh, as the only blemishes appeared where guesses were marked on her side about her empty weight displacement.** This was a mere nine inches, including the four-inch keel. **Frank slipped her into the water with the moves of a man who knows how to handle trailers.** She launched as easy as a rowboat.

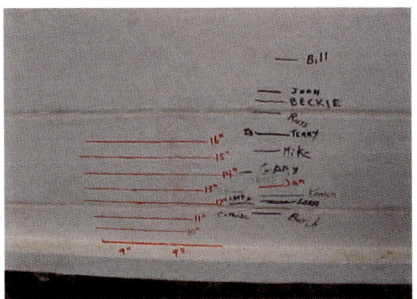

At 6:00 p.m., Butch Bouvier, with the experience of years as a scoutmaster, recommended that we quickly set up camp and begin preparations for the night meal. Even though we didn't end up eating until 9:00, everyone at the camp was excited. The feeling was much like the night before Christmas, when all are filled with anxious an-

ticipation. We set up camp and got acquainted with each other. Many of us were from different walks of life, and even different parts of the country. We all knew we were going on an adventure.

Larry McElroy set up his hawk target stump, which he had fitted with two legs in order to present a better angle to the throw. Many of us took throws at the stump that night and became familiar with our throwing. Larry was already an expert, throwing with one hand or both hands simultaneously. We all turned in early, as we knew that Sunday was rigging day, and we would begin our sea trials with the boat to see how well we worked together.

## Butch Bouvier

### *October 2001*

I keyed in on Tim as a quiet leader early on. I read him as a modest man full of knowledge but not wanting to shove it down anyone's throat. It's hard to believe he is the CEO of a major company. When I found the niche that I thought he would fit well into, I just cut his reins and didn't worry about it any more. Another can-do guy; I just love it!

Tim seemed very impressed with Larry's tomahawk throwing, and I fully expected to see him practicing with Larry's hawks, but never did. I haven't figured that one out yet.

## Butch Bouvier
### 2013

Tim's skill at sailing ended up paying great dividends to the crew. His ability to see a problem and effectively guide the group to a resolution without tipping his hand that he had taken charge of anything was really smooth. Neat. Wish I could pull that off.

# *Day Two: Learning the Ropes*

## Dale
### Sunday, September 30, 2001

Up at 5:00 a.m. and helped cook breakfast in the dark. **As soon as it got light, we began to rig sail.** This was a real learning experience. We worked till about noon to get the sail rigged. The afternoon was spent with the pirogue on the lake. They even did a little sailing under a gentle breeze. When they brought the boat in, Doc decided to go for a little swim—the only problem was he did not have a suit, except for his birthday suit. This did not please the ladies in our ground crew or the ranger at the park. After a short visit from several people, I believe that problem will not occur again. Butch demoted him to Private "parts." We finished the day by doing some programs for the general public. Our first day was successful from a programming point of view. I only hope the rest of the week goes as well.

## Butch Bouvier
### *October 2001*

I would be lying if I didn't say I was disappointed and embarrassed over the skinny-dipping episode. It was an awkward incident for the group. I believe it was just a simple misjudgment by someone far from home.

## Butch Bouvier
### *2013*

We all just loved Doc and Nate, and would have them back in a heartbeat. I guess we all have bad days. These two guys saved our bacon more than once on the river, and we were lucky to have them along.

## Bill
### *Sunday, September 30, 2001*

Made the trip to Ft. Randall mid-afternoon, arriving at 4:30. Saw the boat for the first time, and she's a beauty. Ten-pound cannon was fired once, and I'm sure it could be heard for miles. It will be good to sleep in my own tent tonight after summer trips using troop tents. We were the only ones in the campground, as they were closing for the summer. It's a beautiful area. All seem excited, whether road crew or boat crew. Talk is to get up around 4:00 a.m. to fix breakfast, pack up, and get out on the river.

The anticipation presents the first hint of the excitement that is surely to come over the next five days. It was beautiful day today—70 degrees, and not a cloud in the sky. Foil dinners this evening. They're always great. A huge campfire was built, and several of us enjoyed it after dinner until about 9:30, when we retired for the night, anticipating the early start.

## Butch Bouvier
### *October 2001*

Bill is just a prince of a guy! He got involved early on. When he heard about what I was putting together, he offered to help finance it on behalf of his company. I think Bill came along thinking that he would probably have some fun. I also believe that he sincerely wanted to learn more about the river conditions—and promote his company, as I was mine. But more than that, I think his experience far exceeded anything he expected. I can tell you candidly that I watched him join the group timidly, and by the end of the week he had a hard time leaving for his one-day business trip. I noticed he wasted no time getting back to our group on Friday, and when I saw him for the first time that day, he was smiling from ear to ear.

## Butch Bouvier
### *2013*

I considered it an honor to have spent time with him—a great guy!

## Gary
### *Sunday, September 30, 2001*

This is the day we are to do the final rigging of the boat and take her out for her shakedown cruise. The day started in a scramble for food. Nothing had been planned, so it turned into a potluck using whatever we could scrounge from the members. Becky and I seemed to have planned for breakfast the best, so we supplied most of the meal.

After the meal we went to the lake and ran lines, hung the anchor, and rigged out the sails. **The shakedown trip consisted of two trips around the bay below the face of the dam,** once under power and once under sail. On the way back to shore, Doc Whitaker shucked his cloths and went for a skinny-dip. Of course the park ranger saw the show, and we received a very

severe, "Boys, this is a public park. You cannot be doing this anymore." At supper, things went pretty well, but there was an undercurrent of tension that would stay with the ground crew the entire trip.

## Butch Bouvier
### October 2001

We were quite disorganized at breakfast due to the ground crew members dropping the ball, but the potluck approach worked. I was disappointed in myself and I took the responsibility for the lack of organization. Trying to get everyone moving in the same direction was a challenge. I was the group leader, so I needed to be sure this did not happen again. The tension Gary felt in the air was real, as I felt it also. You just cannot throw this many people together quickly without a few glitches.

## Butch Bouvier
### 2013

The tension Gary talked about was nothing more than personality conflicts. I realize now that everybody was on this trip for different reasons. I have always assumed that all the reasons were honorable, but maybe not quite in sync with my concept of the goals at hand. The group did eventually start to pull together, as my journalists will make note of. Sadly, the goals and standards set by some were not attainable by all.

## Tim
### Sunday, September 30, 2001

Sunday started early at an easy pace. Breakfast was excellent, and we realized that we were going to have to get used to living high on the hog. **Food was delicious and abundant.** It was a beautiful day. Several of us went down to the boat to begin rigging the mast, anchor, and sails. Butch had definite ideas of how he wanted to rig the mast, or as he said, tapping his head with his finger, "I've got it all up here." We began working as a team, with Butch giving us directions on how his ideas would work out in ropes. "Take that to the front of the mast, and then double it and splice it."

**I always enjoyed working with ropes, and I learned quite a bit that day working with Butch.** "Has anybody ever sailed before?" Butch asked. "I have." I said. "Then you're in charge of rigging the sail," Butch instructed. Well, I have never rigged a square-rigger before, but I learned how that day. It  must have turned out OK because it never blew down on our journey. I quickly learned that we had to be careful when we dropped the spar, as it was likely to land on our heads! I also noticed that we didn't have a place to tie off the main halyard.

When I realized there was no cleat for the main halyard, I decided maybe I could fabricate one, since that was what the Lewis and Clark Expedition folks would have had to do. I asked if anyone had a two-by-four, and Frank had an extra piece on the bed of his truck. It was soft and easy to work with, which was fortunate because I did not have any tools. I borrowed Terry's camp saw, shaped the cleat, and finished it with my pocketknife. We screwed it into the mast base, and we had our cleat. The light wood was not up to the task for the whole trip, as it was too soft. But it did do the trick for the moment.

Someone fired off the cannon for the first time as we raised the stars and stripes, and I certainly felt a lump in my throat as I remembered what it was like in Washington DC on Sept. 11th and seeing the Pentagon smoking, but that is another story. I know we all felt a little pride in the undertaking, as we were beginning to relive a small part of our history.

A little later, Willard Dahl and I were finishing up in the boat alone. "Maybe we should fire off the cannon again," I said. "Maybe we should," Willard said. "Have you ever fired a cannon before?" I asked him. "Oh, yeah!" he said. We didn't have a measuring cup, so I held a paper towel in my hands and Willard poured the powder; we put it into the barrel and packed it tightly. I wondered whether we had put in too much powder and I would be killed by shrapnel. We lit the fuse. A loud noise ripped through the park, and Willard and I grinned at each other like five-year-olds that had just set off an M-80.

We went back to camp for some lunch and naps. After lunch, the corps assembled for sea trials. Willard launched his lead boat, and we pushed off. We got out the fifteen homemade oars and began rowing downstream in the basin. It looked like a sword fight as we began. We were taking different lengths of strokes, having the oars in the water at different lengths, and taking short strokes, long strokes, and Armstrong strokes! But we all soon learned to try to coordinate with the person ahead of us so we could see what the stroke was. If we keyed off the last person in the boat, we could all stroke together, or reasonably so.

The oars presented special problems. Being made from rough timber, some were not finely balanced. Some of them had a tendency to lay their flat sides to the water, as that was their natural balance. Those oars found their way to the bottom of the boat. One or two oars had bad spots in them and broke under pressure. By and large the oars were very serviceable, though, and we discovered that a surprising amount of leverage could be extracted due to their long length.

We soon found ourselves in the current of the main channel and could feel the strength of the water accelerating us downstream. We called for Willard and soon had our first lessons in joining a four-ton boat to a two-hundred-pound aluminum boat with a fifteen-horsepower motor. The action and reaction portions of the equation were uneven and led to some interesting situations, most of which involved crewmembers hollering directions for Willard. Having sat (in the chase/towboat) with my hand on the motor handle later in the trip, I gained a lot of appreciation for the difficulty and the concentration that it took. We spent many hours under the towline on a wonderful trip.

As we towed back into the basin again, we hoisted the sail to give it a try, and it worked fine. Boy, was I relieved! As we came back into shore, Nate jumped into the water, and his father soon followed. Although he was so anxious to get in the water that he jumped out of his britches! As we came onto shore, Larry spanked the cannon and made it bark. By this time we had attracted a little crowd that cheered us in. Then Dale and some of the others spread out their artifacts and began our educational sessions. People began to get on the boat for a little tour and to actually feel what it was like to be on a historical pirogue.

Sunday night dinner was hobo meals made in tinfoil. They were delicious, and we enjoyed the feast. Butch passed out the leather-bound journals along with quill pens. He asked us each to maintain a journal of our journey—a journey journal, if you will. Gary, who probably only outweighs me because he is so much taller than I am, started diligently working on his journal with his quill pen and ink by lamplight. I sat down next to him to admire his beautiful penmanship as it covered half of the page. It looked like so much fun that I decided to get up and fetch my journal and get started. As I started to rise, the picnic table lost its balance and began tipping over. Gary had reflexes like a cat and quickly flipped backward, unloading the picnic table. When it stopped tipping, the ink container had spilled across the page of his journal and obliterated his writings. Thereafter, Gary and I always paid close attention to who was on the other side of the table before we sat down. When we were on the pirogue, however, it didn't matter where anyone sat because it was so unbelievably stable.

That night, we all decided to turn in early because we had a lot of miles to cover to be in Lynch, Nebraska, by 9:30 a.m.

## Butch Bouvier

### October 2001

Today was the day I found Tim's niche. He volunteered that he had some sailing experience, and I had the sense he wanted to make suggestions, so I gave him the job. I believe my words were, "It's your cat; you skin it." He didn't hesitate to put people to work, and I immediately knew I had called that one right. I would be willing to bet that when Tim builds his own boat (and I'm sure he will, as he said he wanted to), no matter how small it is, it will have a bow cannon. I can see it now, a twelve-foot johnboat with a twelve-pound cannon mounted on the front. As Gary would say, that would be a hoot! Today was also the day when I believe a friendship started between Tim and Willard Dahl. A CEO of a major company and a county gravel truck driver, two guys from such different walks of life, were playing together like two kids in a mud puddle. And Tim's comments about the size of Willard's boat relative to the *Raycliff* were right on. I have described it as the tail wagging the dog.

## Butch Bouvier

### 2013

A few comments about my friend, Willard Dahl...I count Will as one of my closest friends. On this trip he took more guff and worked harder than any other individual! His positive, shrug-it-off attitude was something I wish I could bottle and force-feed potential riverboat crewmembers. He has more good to say about folks than bad, and that alone makes him stand out as a great guy. Will and I see each other all the time and often talk about this adventure.

# Day Three: Fog and Satisfaction

## Dale
### Monday, October 1, 2001

Butch was beating on the top of my tin tipi at 4:00 a.m. He had already been up and had the fire started. That meant that crazy Butch was up by 3:30. I had breakfast on the fire by 4:15, and by 5:45 we had everyone eating "Dale's delight." By sunup at 6:00 we were on the pirogue. I drove to the noon program on the river near Lynch, Nebraska. This part of things bothers me—we have to pack and drive and get set up to program at noon, and half of the program people are aboard the pirogue. If they are not on time the program will suffer.

Butch had laid out the route so he knew we were going—right—wrong turn, we were in fog, and Butch had led us astray. Butch discovered his mistake, and we all got turned around and headed for our program site. The crew was really in the fog, but that's another story. Our program site was near "Old Baldy" at Sunshine Bottom boat ramp. Sunshine Bottom—BS; it was so foggy near the river you could hardly see.

William Clark wrote of this place on September 7, 1804: "Discovered a village of small animals that burrow in the ground. Caught one live by pouring a great quantity of water in his hole." John Ordway named it the prairie dog. We got to the program site some time before the pirogue made it because of the fog. There were a number of town folks there, and we had lunch started when the pirogue came in. There was a lot of tall grass, weeds, and rocks, and we had been warned about rattlesnakes. So we all bunched up for want of space. Things went well for the first program. The only problem was that a student passed out when Doc did his bloodletting—too real. Doc worked over the introduction and promised there would be no more passing-out problems.

I rode in the pirogue the rest of the day to Niobrara. It was a great ride, and the fall colors in the trees were beautiful. When we got to Niobrara, the guide could not find his way through the backwater channels. We could see Frank's truck, and the ground crew could see our mast, but a few hundred yards of tall water grass with channels dead-ended between us. It could be best described as a maze. We finally worked our way downriver and then back into the main inlet to the landing. We almost got grounded, but the pirogue only needed about eleven inches of water fully loaded. We were over an hour working our way into the dock.

This was a terrible spot for mosquitoes (Clark had seventeen spellings for this word). We had a great elk stew and mosquitoes for supper. Some of the crew went to town to the motel. The rest of us bathed in mosquito repellent and went to bed. Captain Clark would have said the insects "were very troublesome."

## Butch Bouvier

### *October 2001*

Dale is an educator first and foremost, and he was willing, as I was, to pass up time on the boat to make this trip successful. I admire him highly for that. This guy has a way with kids and can hold their attention longer than anyone I have ever known. And with thirty years in the Boy Scouts, I know what I'm talking about. His organizational skills with the kids proved a life-saver, especially when the numbers kept increasing and increasing.

The first school programs at Sunshine bottom were very successful. I must admit that I was a little concerned about the quality of program we would offer. I wasn't worried about Dale, but everyone else was a first-timer at educating. They all did great! And I don't mind telling you that this took a load off my mind. Doc had made his bloodletting (fake) demonstration just a little too realistic, and a kid fainted. I saw the kid go down, and on gravel, to boot! Luckily the young man was not hurt, and Dale and I discussed the problem and decided to ask Doc about taking some precautions, as we were obviously concerned for the children's safety. As it turned out, we discovered what Doc's solution was at the Springfield noon stop the next day. He made sure all the kids were on grass, so they wouldn't get hurt if they fainted! This guy was just a crazy "Kentuckian," and you couldn't help but love him! I did miss the turn to the boat ramp, but found it very shortly. Damn, the fog was bad!

## Butch Bouvier

### 2013

Looking back on it, these first program sessions were just the positive jump start that this expedition needed. Had they been a negative experience, I believe that we would have struggled to attain any level of perfection, let alone even come close to the level we did achieve.

## Bill

### Monday, October 1, 2001

Everyone was up and ready to eat, pack, and get on our way. Doc and Nate slept onboard, and word circulated that the boat was grounded overnight, as the Corps stopped releasing water from the dams overnight. Releases started again around 5:00 a.m., so the boat was out on the river when we reached the dock around 6:00. The ship moved in to get us with Doc and Nate aboard and a heavy fog moving in behind them. It was an eerie sight; like a ghost ship.

Our guide arrived, and Willard finally got his boat started, so we all boarded the white pirogue newly named the *Raycliff*. We were no more than a couple hundred yards from shore when the cannon was fired. I'm guessing several people in Pickstown started their workweek awakening to that explosion.

The fog was dense all around us almost immediately, so we decided to move very cautiously until the sun rose and burned it off. Unfortunately that was not to be. The fog stayed with us all morning, and a lot of the material beauty along this stretch of the river was missed. At one point our guide, Willard, and the pirogue got all turned around. We were headed back up the river without even noticing until a compass was consulted, and the situation was quickly corrected. We hooked up to Willard's boat and accepted a tow the rest of the morning until docking at Lynch, Nebraska, for our first school program.

Quite a few students and other townspeople turned out, and all seemed to enjoy themselves. The crew enjoyed some wonderful pastries and coffee while at dock. Old Baldy was in clear view once the fog finally burned off, and everyone admired it through binoculars or telescopic lenses on cameras. Each crewmember received a nice sack lunch, and we departed for Niobrara around noon. The weather was now beautiful with full sunshine.

The wind would not cooperate, and we could not sail, so we rowed and were towed through the afternoon. It was a long day, covering close to forty miles of the river. The photographers in the group made up for lost time under full sunshine and took pictures from the pirogue and from Willard's boat all afternoon. We began to attract attention, and several boats came close to check us out. On at least a couple of occasions, our cannoneer, Larry, greeted them with a blast from the cannon. He always preceded the explosion with the warning shout, "Fire in the hole!" We even exchanged cannon fire with a group of people sitting at their cottage. Their dog must have been familiar with similar routines, as he ran as soon as he heard the shouting. We took a short stop for a cool beverage late in the afternoon, and we carried an elderly couple from that dock to theirs—a short distance downstream.

When we finally reached Niobrara, we spent some time figuring out the correct way to port through all the small channels. The people onshore could see our mast, but we could not see them. After talking to Butch on the radio, we determined it would be best to go about a half-mile downstream and then back up a small channel to our destination. This was the hardest work of the day. **With Captain Mike Butler firmly in control on the rudder/sweep, we manned the oars and literally pulled ourselves all the way up that channel, as it was very shallow.** I was sweating heavily by the time we docked.

While Butch and a few others enlightened our visitors on the boat's features, I immediately set up my tent while the sun went down and hordes of mosquitoes came out of the surrounding grass. By the light of lanterns, we enjoyed a marvelous dinner of elk stew and homemade bread. I ate quickly and was in my tent and asleep by 8:30. Apparently most of the others retired shortly thereafter or breezed into town to a comfortable room and a shower.

A wonderful, interesting, long, and diverse first day. Thank God we're going downstream! Lewis and Clark and their crew must have been exalted by what they saw along this great river, but exhausted each evening by the effort they had to put in, especially going up the river.

## Butch Bouvier

### *October 2001*

While waiting for the boat to arrive at the morning stop, I grew very concerned. **My baby and my crew were out there, and I couldn't see my hand in front of my face.** I was so relieved when I heard someone hollering, "They're here!" Then in the distance I could just make out, "Fire in the hole!" I would describe it as a voice way off in a fog bank, but that would be way too accurate. What was really neat was when the cannon went off. The concussion blew a hole in the fog, no kidding, just like special effects in the movies. "Too cool" is the only way to describe it.

At one point Catherine asked Dale if there was anything she could do to help. **He handed her a thirty-pound flintlock rifle and told her to guard the boat ramp.** I have never figured out if she thought he was serious or just did it for fun, but she shouldered this antique monster and took off for the ramp. She got a little close to the water's edge and stepped in some wet moss, lost her footing, and went down in a clump. She immediately picked herself and her "cannon" up and continued; she's a real trooper!

The next big water adventure would come at Niobrara. Our communications had broken down, and the boat was behind schedule. My wife Catherine and I, along with Buffalo Bill, resolved that we would keep the crowd occupied until the boat arrived. When we were just about out of material, we spotted the mast above the river grass, but it was obvious they had missed the channel. I made connection with them via cell phone and told them to go downstream to the second channel. A local guy standing next to me said, "Don't do that," but it was too

late. So I asked him to explain, figuring that if I had to, I would hire a boat to go after them. He said that no one used that channel except airboats, as it was only about nine inches deep. He then asked me how big our boat was. When I told him it was forty-two feet long and seven thousand pounds, he said that I should immediately

get someone out there to get them back upstream to the main inlet. I did some quick calculations and told him that they could make it with luck. He just shook his head and walked away. **I didn't see his face when they came up that channel, but I'd bet he was quite surprised.**

## Butch Bouvier
### 2013

Cathy and I have talked about this first day many times. It seems that her falling with the rifle, the hole in the fog, and the mosquitoes dominate the conversation. I have told her over the years that Dale had a picture of her in a heap on the boat ramp, and that I was going to use it in the book. The word *divorce* comes into the conversation every time, so I drop the subject. By the way, Dale never took that picture, but I haven't told her that yet.

## Gary
### Monday, October 1, 2001

We were all up at 4:00 a.m., chomping at the bit. After a hearty breakfast, it was off to the *Raycliff* for launch. The water had gone down and left our chase boat nearly ten feet above the waterline. After dragging it back into the water, we had to wait for our river pilot. We shoved off from shore, and with my first stroke my oar broke. We ended up breaking a total of three during the first day and a half. So much for using honey locust full of knots and carpenter ants. Once underway, it took about fifteen minutes to be totally immersed in a thick, unrelenting river fog. It was so dense that often we could not see our river guide or our support boat. Upon trying to contact Willard in the support boat, we found out our communication system was not working, and it refused to work for the entire trip.

As the fog thickened, even the guide boat got lost, and we started back up the river. We had to shut the trip down until we could see the horizon. We waited about a half hour before we could start. Finally we could just barely make out the tops of the trees, so we headed for Lynch, Nebraska. Willard had to pull us most of the way so we could make it to the training event on time. As we approached the landing, the fog set back in, and we nearly shot past the landing. With instruction from Doc, we were able to make a safe landing without any problems. We had at least a hundred school kids at the landing, and the session went very well. They fed us some sandwiches and sweet rolls, and then sent us on our way to Niobrara, Nebraska. (I hate this quill pen!)

We were able to do a little sailing on the way downstream to Niobrara. As we reached the Niobrara landing area, our river guide sent us to the wrong channel. We had to back the boat into the main channel and hang on to the tall river grass to keep from being carried downstream until we regained control. When the guide finally found the channel, it was too shallow for his boat. The *Raycliff* was able to make it fine. Of course, the wind failed us again, and we had to turn to the oars. We had a nice reception and a meal of very tasty elk stew. The mosquitoes were so bad that nearly half the crew gave up the comfort of the tents and forced themselves to endure the hardship of a local motel. My wife and me, the Butlers, and the McElroys went to a local saloon that was decorated in old west style. They had various animal heads hanging on the walls and two rattlesnake skins. These skins had to be six or seven feet long and were very impressive. As it turned out, we found out who had provided our wonderful meal at the landing. Becky recognized the lady who owned the ranch that supplied the elk meat for the stew. She worked out a deal to take a tour for free the next morning.

## Butch Bouvier
### October 2001

I should make some comments about the oars. Dale had said earlier that he was just so impressed that I had the boat done on time. But he didn't know that I did rob from Peter to pay Paul a little, and our inadequate communications and sadly made oars were the result of that. Next time she goes out, the oars will be perfect, and the radios will be able to talk to Moscow if we need them to!

## Butch Bouvier
### 2013

The next time we went out, we had very good oars and a motor, so the oars weren't needed much. Gary and his family really gave this adventure their all. Good attitude and committed effort with no complaining!

Too shallow for the guide boat, but not for my girl...who says modern-day design is always better?

## Tim
### Monday, October 1, 2001

Butch and Dale turned out to be our alarm clocks and showed their experience at camping by laughing and talking boisterously and beginning to get the camp on the move. Dale showed his experience with Dutch ovens by whipping up omelets for us in the campfire. **He said that anyone who can count to three could use a Dutch oven.**

We sent someone down with rations for Nate and Doc. They had slept on the boat and anchored it out in the bay, as we were all concerned about the overnight water level due to the dam discharge rate being drastically lowered at overnight. We broke camp and headed down to the river by 5:30 a.m. to discover that they were anchored to a buoy in midstream and had not been aroused by the folks onshore with their breakfast.

Some new members to our party had joined us overnight, including a *Nebraskaland* photographer. Willard's boat was about twenty-five feet high and dry, and several of us began to drag it back to the water so we could launch it. We finally had it most of the way into the water when Willard jumped in, and we pushed him off. There wasn't a breath of air moving or any current we could notice as Willard drifted out into the bay, pulling and pulling on the motor's starter rope to try and get it started. The pirogue arrived at shore under oar power, and we began to load. Meanwhile Willard, having planned ahead, dug out new spark plugs and installed them in his motor and was able to get it running. A guy who lived in the area arrived and launched his boat as well. He was familiar with this stretch of the river, as he lived only about fifteen miles downstream. As the gray of dawn arrived, so did the fog; we knew we would not be sailing that morning. We all loaded as quickly as we could, pushed off downriver, and waved good-bye to our shore party. The oars came out, and we again began our lessons in coordination, only this time in the fog. The fog grew heavier, and at times we lost sight of our guide. We began to cross a shallow bar, which was surprisingly very rocky. For a couple of moments I felt as if we were running rapids. Then we were in the main channel again, and we were shouting from boat to boat to keep our bearings on each other. At one point, we realized the guide had gone upriver and none of us were sure of our directions, so I reached into my bag and consulted a compass to see what direction we were actually heading. It turned out we were headed upstream, so we got turned around and proceeded on. The fog became more patchy, visibility improved slightly, but we were still unable to see most of the riverbank along that stretch. I rigged my pack rod and began fishing from the stern. After about a half hour of trolling, I caught a smallmouth bass, but I didn't think he would go very far to feed the group, so I released him and gave fishing a rest.

As the fog began lifting we crossed the Nebraska border and now have Nebraska on the southern shore. The Missouri is the boundary from here to Sioux City between South Dakota and Nebraska. We soon came upon Sunshine Bottom, which I had heard of but had never seen before. It was a lovely stretch of river—what we could see of it through the fog.

Not far from there, we came upon the boat landing at Lynch, where **we were welcomed with a flare and our loyal ground crew, as well as a sizable crowd of folks from the area.** Larry fired off the cannon to announce our arrival; the boat was swinging

around and did a one-eighty, so the cannon was pointing right over the people's heads onshore. Mike did a great job of landing the boat on the Nebraska side of the river, and we all got out to stretch our legs.

**Dale portrayed Sgt. Gass** with his memorable artifacts from the era, including the lead powder flasks and the tooth-extraction equipment. He also had some of Dr. Rush's thunderbolts, which looked like puppy chow. Larry demonstrated hawk-throwing, and Doc looked for a volunteer to show the bloodletting procedure, which was noted at the time

to cure just about anything. This demonstration caused at least one lad to faint away! I went back to the pirogue during this time and looked into the water and saw a large school of minnows about six feet deep, playing in the current. The water was incredibly clear and not like the Missouri River around Sioux City.

We were well fed with Danish rolls and elephant tracks (or elephant ears, depending on what part of the country you are in), coffee, sandwiches, and fresh-picked apples.

While we were there, the fog lifted, leaving a bright, sunny day and a beautiful view of the river and Old Baldy on the hillside. Butch had made contact with the folks who owned the property that Old Baldy sits on and began a dialog with them about the future of this historical site along the Lewis and Clark Trail. Old Baldy is where Lewis and Clark were introduced to the prairie dog and went to some effort to capture one alive. This original dog still exists in Virginia, at Jefferson's Monticello.

We were extremely relieved when we left Lynch landing, as we had met our morning deadline and were at the landing when we were supposed to be. The photographer from *Nebraskaland* magazine had been with us all morning and had taken numerous pictures. During the downriver run that morning, he and Dale had compared notes, and they found they had many acquaintances in common. We left Lynch landing and continued downstream, enjoying the many beautiful sites and relaxed atmosphere. We continued to fire off the cannon to make sure we did not sneak up on any wildlife, and occasionally a boater would return our salute. As we approached the village of Verdel, we noticed a large cannon onshore. We had already loaded our cannon in preparation for a salute to the town when the man onshore hollered, "Fire in the Hole!" We quickly lit our cannon, and we must have had a shorter fuse, as ours went off before his. This man's dog must have been very familiar with the routine, because when he shouted, the dog ran and hid under the house. We all had a good laugh at that.

We arrived at Verdel landing and caught a ride to the nearest bar to replenish our fluids before quickly returning to the boat. As we were loading the boat, Doc offered a ride to some local residents who lived about ten miles downstream. They appeared to be in their eighties, but they were game and certainly did enjoy the trip.

As we approached Niobrara, I began to see parts of the river that were familiar to me. I think the farthest upstream I had ever been was across from the mouth of the Niobrara River. As you pass the mouth of the Niobrara, you can distinguish its muddy water from the color of the Missouri in that area. We were given instructions to pull into the first channel after passing the mouth of the Niobrara, which would lead into the landing at Niobrara. However, as we came upon it, it appeared to be too small to lead to the boat ramp, so we pushed out and went on to the second channel, which had a substantial current. We could make out what we figured was the boat ramp about a half a mile away due to the tops of vehicles showing above the tall river grass. The second channel was soon found to be a dead end, so we took a chance and went on downstream looking for another way in. We finally came upon a very shallow channel heading back upstream to the boat ramp about six hundred yards ahead and decided to try it. We scraped bottom a few times, but with much effort by everyone, we eventually arrived with a cannon salute and cheers from the crowd of over one hundred people. We were one and a half hours late; it was 6:30.

As we began unloading, I looked over the crowd for some of my many relatives who lived in the Verdel and Niobrara area. I noticed a lovely young woman with jet-black hair with recognition in her eyes. As I walked up to her, I knew that she was the daughter of a long time employee. We chatted awhile before she had to leave. The crowd quickly thinned as mosquitoes came out in droves.

We quickly divided into two groups: those who would camp for the evening and those who would go to the motel in town. We had an elk stew and sausage dinner served with a wild rice casserole; all of which were great. I found that after I sprayed with mosquito repellent the fourth time, the mosquitoes no longer bothered me, and I was very grateful. Campfire conversations ended quickly, and we retired to the safety of our tents. The local paperboy delivered the day's paper, so I caught up with things in my tent before I went to bed.

## Butch Bouvier
### October 2001

Our late arrival at Niobrara was a close call. As it turned out, it would not be our last late arrival. I had been concerned from the beginning that my schedule was too aggressive, and it turned out to be true. The crew tried as hard as they could to keep on schedule, but I was asking too much of them. I could see them beginning to knit together, and Mike's leadership skills were starting to show. All in all, we were to this point pretty successful. We had one fantastic kid's program and one evening adult program, which went well even if it started later than planned. The worst parts of this day were the stinking pit toilets, which smelled so foul you almost puked, and the mosquitoes. I don't believe I have ever seen them this bad.

## Butch Bouvier
### 2013

Ugh! Memories of those awful mosquitoes.

# Day Four: A Long, Hard Day

## Dale
### Tuesday, October 2, 2001

I met with Butch before 5:00 a.m. and talked about the programs and the crew. I told Butch that I had been watching Frank, and he had expressed some interest in trying to talk to the people at the pirogue. I planned on working with him on a first-person role of Corporal Worfington, who was in charge of the white pirogue on the way up the river and brought the keelboat down the river the following spring. I think Butch thought I was crazy. I led the ground crew overland to Springfield, South Dakota. Butch had lined up a lady as a river guide for the crewmembers, and they had no problems with the sandbars off Springfield. We had an excellent place to set up for programs. The only problem was that we were about done with the programs when another three buses full of kids showed up. One of the biggest headaches we had was never knowing for sure how many kids were going to be at noon programs. This time it put us back on the water over an hour late. We had a lot of media coverage at Springfield, and we even put one of them onboard for the afternoon run down the lake.

As we hit Lewis and Clark Lake, we encountered heavy head winds. Butch had arranged for a large and powerful towboat, as he knew we were well behind schedule and the sun would set by 6:00 p.m. At one point, we had waves coming over the bow of the boat. Even the large towboat was having trouble, and Willard's small boat was lashed to the side of the pirogue, as it was deemed to risky for him to stay in it. We had to take the pirogue out at the dam and portage around before we could continue to Yankton.

Frank Koeppe and his truck-driving skills really paid off on this one. After putting back in, we started down the river to Yankton. The sun set, but the moon was full. We had picked up a new guide who couldn't find his nose in a windstorm. He took us to the wrong side of the river and got us into a large mass of dead trees. It was like a war movie, watching torpedoes coming at you out of the dark, except it was dead tree branches, not weapons. We turned tail and went like crazy to get clear of them.

We crossed the river to the South Dakota side; it was after 10:00 p.m. before we got to Riverside Park in Yankton, South Dakota. When we were getting off the pirogue, Larry went down on us. He had been about ten hours without food, and his sugar was screwed up. I found some people on the dock with some old brownies with frosting and scraped off the frosting for Larry. In a few minutes, we had him back; thank God it didn't happen on the river.

It was a long but good day, and it was great to see the crew come together on the water in the mass of torpedo trees, where we had to all work together instantly to avert a disaster. It has taken a couple of days, but we have jelled.

## Butch Bouvier
### October 2001

Dale's attempt to turn a middle-aged trucker onto a valid programmer was what I considered to be a study in futility. As it eventually turned out, it was a success in two areas. Dale transformed Frank Koeppe into Cpl. Richard Worfington, and he also created a monster…a likable monster, and an unpredictable one.

I had seriously misjudged the time frame for that day's travels. It put the boat and the crew at risk, and in particular had endangered Larry's health. This ate on me most of that evening. And my poor planning would have continued to mess with my mind the next day, but I knew I didn't have time to distress over it. So I shook it off and plunged ahead in the morning.

## Butch Bouvier
### 2013

That next morning was a turning point for the expedition. Some of the personality conflicts boiled over, and try as I might, I could not seem to get them resolved. Larry regained his strength quickly, and everyone was ready to go. At least the personality problems were not affecting my boat crew. Twelve years later, it's easy to say that the problems with my ground crew were no big deal. But at the time, they were eating me up. It would eventually be resolved when some of our ground crew had to break off early and head home. It takes two to tango, and this broke up the party, so there was no more dancing.

## Bill
### Tuesday, October 2, 2001

We arose around 6:00 a.m. in the dark and cooked breakfast. The day was predicted to be hot, but clear. No fog today! We were on our way by 9:00 a.m., and were able to put up the sails and enjoy the ride. The river is quite complicated for several miles where the Niobrara meets the Missouri. The siltation is incredible, and we were thankful for our guide Sandy, whom Nate quickly renamed "Sandy-ja-wia." Mike continued steering the boat masterfully and yelling at the rest of us when he needed "our power!"

A huge crowd of school children awaited us at Springfield, and we spent four hours docked there giving demonstrations, visiting with a reporter from the *Sioux City Journal*, and eating lunch. I spent a delightful hour lying on a hillside above the docked boat visiting with three old-timers from the community. They told me how there was a college in town that finally closed and was converted to a state prison the same year. That was around 1984, I believe. They also reminisced about how beautiful this part of the river was back in the 1950s and early 1960s, before the sedimentation buildup became a serious and noticeable problem. Now there are reasonably large trees growing on some of the areas of silt deposits, and the river's beauty is gone until several miles further downstream.

The presentations given to the children are quite impressive. Gary gives a different presentation each time, depending on the age and knowledge level of the kids. Dale is in full uniform as Patrick Gass, and he has many stories about the men of the Lewis and Clark Expedition. He also uses a considerable array of items as props. His extensive knowledge makes the presentations first-rate. Larry entertained the kids with his tomahawk throwing, and of course all the kids got to try their luck at it. Doc and Nate discussed the medical techniques of the time, highlighted by a realistic demonstration of how a person was "bled." A couple of kids got woozy at what they thought was real blood, but I never tire of the presentation.

Finally we were back on the river under sail, but that was not to last, as we were seriously behind schedule for our evening programs in Yankton, so we accepted a tow through Lewis and Clark Lake. The lake is much larger than I had thought, but we were fortunate that the breeze was fairly light, making for a comfortable crossing. The South Dakota side was extremely good habitat for bald eagles along this stretch, and we saw many of these majestic birds. This was a stretch of the trip where I enjoyed lengthy conversations with Dale, Terry, Doc, and Robbie, and I got to know each of them much better. We finally reached Gavins Point Dam around 6:00 p.m. It was an exciting time loading the boat, portaging around the dam, and putting it back into the water just before sunset at an extremely narrow, steep, and unforgiving boat ramp. Frank did a splendid job leading that whole process and showing off his skills in that regard. We were once again underway, but it was now dark, and we enjoyed the vision of a magnificent full moon. While we all leaned overboard to enjoy the sight and a wonderful fall evening, we hung up on a log. With help from our guide boat, we quickly dislodged it and continued on to Yankton. More excitement was still to follow. The famous "over/under bridge" at Yankton was quickly approaching, and it was impossible to tell if we would clear it with our mast up. With flashlights focused on the top of the mast, we cleared the bridge with what seemed to be only a few feet. Certainly that was not an obstacle that Lewis and Clark had to deal with, but we were extremely relieved our encounter was only one of uncertainty and not one of destruction of the mast!

As we docked at Yankton, we were amazed to find quite a few people still waiting for us, even though we were more than three hours late. Larry experienced a diabetic reaction, and we quickly got a brownie popped into him. We enjoyed a nice chicken dinner under the shelter at Riverside Park, and I reluctantly bid everyone farewell until my return on Thursday, as I had some business at work to attend to. The drive home was long, as I was quite tired from a couple of long days. I reached home at 11:30 p.m., placed my dirty clothes in a pile, and settled down for a short night's sleep. But at least I was in my own comfortable bed!

## Butch Bouvier

### *October 2001*

OK, Bill, were you on the same boat as the rest of the guys? "A pleasant crossing" is I believe how you described it. And then while they were groping their way through the dark trying to find the dock and avoid tree trunks, you were admiring the wonderful moon. Yes, Bill was on the same boat, and I am not surprised that he saw things differently than the others. If you read the expedition journals, you will see many instances of this discrepancy between what individuals perceived at the same time and in the same place.

## Butch Bouvier

### *2013*

I like this passage. I think it displays how our perspective on something is at least partially governed by our basic approach to it. If you perceive it as a challenge, you're looking for challenges. If you perceive it as a great adventure, then it is.

# Gary
### Tuesday, October 2, 2001

The plan for this day was to arrive at the boat ramp well before dawn to eat our breakfast, meet the river guide for day number two, and then hit the water. After breakfast we waited and waited for our river guide to show. Young lady finally arrived and said that if it would be OK, she would be our substitute river guide. Her boyfriend had been our original guide, but his parents had been in a serious accident, and he needed to be with them. She said that she had been over that section of the river many times with her boyfriend. She was also the city administrator for Springfield, South Dakota, and that was to be our first stop of the day. Her first name was Sandy, so she was immediately dubbed "Sandy-ja-wia," as she was our female guide, just like Lewis and Clark. She and Elaine went to the bow of the boat, and Sandy-ja-wia would relay back to Mike where he needed to be in the river channel.

Our first challenge was to negotiate a group of sandbars and still be in the correct channel to get aligned to run under a new bridge. Willard was helping tow, and of course our communications system had not worked from the outset, so it was hard for him to know where we needed him to take us. Plus the weight of the pirogue would make his boat go off-line. This often made us travel in a crisscross pattern and earned him the nickname "Wandering Willie." With all this in mind, Sandy wanted Willard to take us on the starboard side of a sandbar. Willard couldn't get us lined up; the pirogue did a front-to-rear swap, and it was all men on deck! Doc and Nate gave directions as to which side needed to row and in what direction. We rowed like crazy, and at times were in such shallow water we were pulling up grass off the river bottom. We were very pleased with ourselves when we realized we had made it around our first challenge and had maneuvered the boat against and through a strong current and no one had been hurt. We then hooked back onto Willard and headed for the bridge. He had to take us across current to get us lined up for the bridge pillars. We don't know if he turned with the current too soon, or if the current grabbed him and the pirogue, or what; anyway, we whipped toward the pillar so hard and fast that Mike had to pull the tiller out of the way at the last minute. We could not have missed the bridge by more than one or two inches. Our little "expedition" came very close to ending at the bottom of that bridge.

Soon after the bridge, we were able to set sail and cut Willard away again. With instructions from Tim and Doc, we were able to sail the rest of the way to Springfield. We found that by playing the wind just right, we could sideslip around many of the curves in the channel and miss the sandbars and the many small islands that determine the course of the river at Springfield. We used the oars as bumpers when we strayed too close to the banks, and in this manner we proceeded on without hanging up or losing any speed. We dropped sail, and made a 180-degree pivot with the boat into the basin Springfield uses as a boat launch, just as the first buses were pulling into the picnic area. This was the best timing we experienced for the whole trip. When we look back on the trip, it dawned on us that Sandy was the only guide we had that never ran us aground or lost the channel. Hats off to women!

I think all of us had an excellent time at Springfield, especially with the kids. As the buses were leaving, we could hear the children doing the military cheer, which I had taught them. We also got great press coverage and a large article in the *Sioux City Journal*.

The groups of kids were so large that we left Springfield behind schedule, and we really had no idea how long it would take to go all the way down the lake and take out at Gavins Point Dam. We sailed for a little while, and then decided to hook onto a towboat to make better time. We used Willard for a while, but it became apparent that he could not handle it and it wasn't safe for him, as we were being hit broadside by a heavy wind. We had fairly heavy waves to fight, and without that big boat out front, we were forced to shore. The ride down the lake was choppy, but the view was wonderful. At one point, we had a group of horses running along the shore, keeping up with us. At some point on the lake, Wayne started looking a little peaked, but of course he wouldn't tell anyone if he felt well or not. As we got further down the lake, the wind calmed, and we took advantage by having nice visits and catching up on some naps. The reporter was getting a little concerned that since we were behind schedule she would miss her ride back to Sioux City.

We arrived at the takeout point, loaded the boat on the trailer, and made our way past the dam. We put in OK and hired a man and his son to tow us to the next program point in Yankton. We were now roughly two hours past our scheduled time and started pushing safety and ourselves a little bit. We starting heading downstream by flashlight. Of course we ended up in the wrong channel. When we realized our mistake, we were in a land mine of sawyers, deadfalls, and shallow water. Once again, our guide had led us astray. He turned his boat around and pulled us into and up on a large snag. We used the oars to try to push off the snag, but had to resort to shifting the load in the boat to get free. As soon as were we off that snag, we got hung up on a sandbar. At this point, I can honestly say that I was concerned about the safety of the crew. When we finally worked our way back to the correct channel, our next obstacle was the double-decker highway bridge. No one knew how tall our mast was or how low the bridge's lower deck was. We made ready to lower the mast in a hurry, just in case we wouldn't clear. Fortunately we had plenty of room.

It then became apparent that our landing was close at hand and no one had set a flare or any other type of signal for us. At this point we became a non-working unit and did not do ourselves proud. We started yelling at the towboat all at once, and the poor man really had no idea where we wanted to go. I felt we were embarrassing ourselves in front of the locals, so I hollered out, " Damn it! Everyone shut up! He can only listen to one at a time!" It got deathly quiet. Then I saw a man on a deck overhanging the river, so I asked him if he knew where our landing was. He told us it was less than a quarter mile downstream. We made our landing safely, and out towboat made a hasty retreat back upriver. I must say, I don't blame him at all. We started to clean up the deck and secure the ropes. The Yanktonians had waited a long time, and the children were chomping at the bit and could hardly wait to get onboard. As I started to leave, I noticed Larry just standing with one foot on the deck and one on the dock. I asked him if he was OK, and he did not respond. I then put my hand on his back and noted that he was cold, sweaty, and clammy all over. I knew his history and surmised he was having trouble with his blood sugar. I called for Mike, and we got Larry off the boat and onshore. People in our way thought we were being rude, but when we told them we had a sick man, they became very helpful—offering candy, chocolate, etc. By the time Larry's wife showed up, he was well on his way to recovery. Becky and Carolyn then made sure that Larry was well taken care of. The boat crew went ahead and gave a program onboard, and I think the people who stayed around were fairly well placated.

My wife and I spent the night in a local motel because we did not want to make camp after dark and strike camp before the sun came up. Plus two different groups of locals had told us that the next day would be the most challenging that we would face on the river. It's kind of funny, but each town had at least one person who just had to say the next part would be the hardest part.

## Butch Bouvier

### October 2001

Gary always sees the positive side of things, so when he got stern with the crew, I am assuming that things were pretty ugly. Good for him!

## Butch Bouvier

### 2013

Gary was a damned good wooden spoon over a pot of boiling potatoes. Too bad he couldn't have stayed around longer.

## Tim

### Tuesday, October 2, 2001

The next morning was another beautiful day, and we launched with Sandy from the city office in Springfield as our guide. She had been up and down the river numerous times with her boyfriend and was a last-minute stand-in when his parents were injured in a car accident. Nate quickly dubbed her Sandy-ja-wia, and she was our able-bodied guide for the day. As we set off downriver, we went by the landing where the Running Water ferry used to load passengers and automobiles on the Nebraska side to ferry over to the South Dakota side. It was one of the last ferries on the central Missouri River and was owned by relatives of mine.

We hoisted the sail and found that the wind was blowing from the southwest. However, we drifted a little too far to the north and found ourselves on the north side of the river, but we wanted to go under the bridge on the south side. We were carried this way by the sail. We struck the sail and put out the oars and made it back across the stream to the south side. We gave the towrope to Willard, and he towed us under the bridge, missing the bridge abutment by three feet. I saw the expression on Mike Butler's face!

We then went by the landing on the running-water side. Sandy told us about the local bar owner who would come down to the landing to pick up people from boats in order to sell them beer. We enjoyed floating down the river, and we saw our first bald eagle sitting in a tree. At long last, we reached the bluffs on the Nebraska side of the river, and the river curved more to the east. We raised the sail for a very exhilarating ride into Springfield. We sailed down the river until Sandy led us into the chute, which cuts back across the river to the north. This leads to the Springfield basin. We were able to sail down the narrow chute, and we made great speed with both the current and the sail working in tandem. Rather than tying off the spar braces, Frank stood in the back of the boat by the sweep with a rope in both hands and learned to adjust the sail to catch the wind and maximize our propulsion. It looked like he was reining in some airborne horses rather than airborne horsepower.

On the bluffs in Springfield overlooking the chute, a World War I cannon overlooks the river in the small park. As we approached, we could see our ground crew on the bluff, and we were happy when they saluted us with Larry's cannon. We responded with our cannon as we sailed triumphantly into the basin. We tied up in their first-class landing facilities, and the women made a beeline for the local facilities. Our wonderful traveling companions amazed me.

We had a delicious lunch as we waited for our students to arrive. We did not have to wait long. We were soon inundated with students from many schools. We even had students from different districts, and in order to keep some semblance of order, we used the boat as a marshaling area to hold one school while we finished up with another. We had Gary teaching celestial navigation, Doc with his bloodletting, Larry with his hawk-throwing, and Dale as Sgt. Gass for the different stations. **We rotated every fifteen minutes, when Robbie would fire his rifle.**

Butch gave the first presentation with the students on the boat, and I listened in close attention because every time I heard one of his demonstrations I learned something new. After he finished, he would invite the students to file past the sweep at the stern of the boat and grab hold of it and move it back and forth and lift it out of the water to get a feel for what it took to steer the boat. Afterward he asked me if I had been listening. When I answered in the affirmative, he said, "Great, 'cause you're giving the next one. Got to see a man about a horse. Have fun!" I was initially apprehensive at the thought. I can address a thousand of my peers at a convention with only mild butterflies, but holding the attention of a bunch of children was not something I had experience with. I know they can be a tough audience. As the students were filing onboard, mostly third and fourth graders, one of the teachers brought over a microphone and a small transmitter, which would transmit and amplify my voice to a young boy with hearing difficulties. With my own hearing loss, I felt a special mission at that point.

As I launched into my presentation, I repeated a lot of what Butch said. I also included some information I had gleaned through the other presentations as well as my readings. I was able to maintain their attention for quite a while; of course the teachers were there to lend a hand! During the second presentation, I began to wonder if I was repeating myself or if it was some-

thing I had just told the first group. It was very rewarding to tell these kids things they hadn't thought about before. I could see their minds opening up to the new ideas by the questions they asked. **Frank took the next group, as my voice was getting hoarse.**

Both reporters and photographers were at the Springfield stop, and the reporter boarded with us for the trip down to the Lewis and Clark Lake. We left the Springfield basin about 3:30 p.m. and promptly hoisted the sail, as we were due at the Yankton City Park at 5:30 for a presentation. This also involved loading the pirogue back onto the trailer, trucking it around the dam, and launching it below the dam. We took a tow from a bass boat, as we knew we had to make up a lot of lost time. The lake became somewhat rough as a wind continued to blow from the northwest at about fifteen miles per hour. It would have been a great sail if we had had the time. I think there was some snake oil remedy making the rounds in the boat, but I passed, as I hadn't seen any snakes.

We finally made it to the head of the dam just as it was getting dark. We took ropes out on either side of the boat and used them to steady her as we loaded her on the trailer. We were able to load up without too much trouble, which was good, as we were in a great hurry. We loaded up in the vehicles for the ride around the dam. A couple others and I rode with the South Dakota game warden, who was from Nebraska originally and was starting his second season in this position. I think he was as thrilled to be with the party on this portion of the journey as we were.

We went to the boat landing below the dam and found that we were in the middle of spoonbill season. The ramp was quite steep and narrow, and Frank was a little nervous about getting the trailer back up the ramp. He masterfully backed the boat down the narrow ramp with mere inches to clear on either side in one smooth pass. We talked to a boater at the ramp who agreed to be our guide for the next few miles down to the Yankton City Park. We quickly loaded and headed out, as it was already dark. The trip went fine for the first mile, until we came to some standing pilings on the right-hand side of the river, which is where we should've crossed to the north side of the river. However, our guide led us straight down the middle, and we soon began dodging logs sticking out in the middle of the river. Soon thereafter we saw his outdrive kick up some sand, and he tossed the towrope to us. We were on our own! We put the oars in and worked our way out of that mess so we could get back into safe water on the South Dakota side.

We continued in the dark, but we could see some lovely homes along the river and a lot of black water. We soon had other things to think about as we came upon the Highway 81 bridge. There were some anxious moments as we shined flashlights on the mast and the bridge as we slipped under it with room to spare. We were now hot on the lookout for the dock at the city park, but none of us knew where it was. There were some more anxious moments until it came into sight. The wind was coming up stronger, and we were in a hurry to get docked, establish camp, and eat some supper. Many people were on the dock to see the pirogue. Our shore party was arriving about the same time as we did. On top of all this, we had a medical emergency, which further put everyone on edge.

We sat down to a delicious dinner of fried chicken, baked beans, and all the trimmings—lots of it. With the food, the warmth of the lamps, and the camaraderie, the tension just melted away from us. The wind continued to blow and even picked up speed. Before long it was blowing about twenty-five miles per hour, with gusts to forty. Putting up the tents became a challenging effort, and several of the party chose to take motel rooms. Those of us who continued with our camping efforts worked together and helped one another get set up. We had Frank place his semi in front of camp as a windbreak. I remember standing dumbfounded as the wind flattened my tent just after I had finished putting it up. The addition of my rainfly added just enough structural integrity to prevent this from happening again. I guess rainflies aren't just for rain.

## Butch Bouvier
### October 2001

Tim stepped right up to the programming plate. Heck, I sort of thrust it upon him, so he had no choice. But he did very well! Our new Worfington followed him and did pretty well himself.

## Butch Bouvier
### 2013

The high point for this day was Frank Koeppe doing his first full-boat program. He was sweating like a hog, but he got through it. Now, twelve years later, all I have to do is mention a program, and he goes into Worfington mode!

# Day Five: An Easier Day

## Dale
### Wednesday, October 3, 2001

Up at 4:30 and had pancakes, and I cooked "little smokies" in the Dutch oven. We were on the water shortly after 6:00 a.m. Today was a cooler day than we have had. We didn't have a noon program today, so we just floated along with the current. Some of the fellows broke out their guns and did some live firing. We saw a lot of wildlife—deer, turkeys, beaver runs, hawks, eagles, blue heron, and sea gulls. We wanted to stop on an island for lunch like Lewis and Clark would have done, but we could not find a suitable one. We eventually stopped along the bank and had lunch. It was very enjoyable to eat on the bank along this magnificent river. Terry went to get his tripod and camera so we could get a group picture. He stood the tripod up in Willard's small aluminum chase boat and stepped ashore. After retrieving the camera from the water, we decided to skip the group picture, as if we had any choice. Shortly after lunch, we grounded hard on a sandbar. Using poles and shifting our load, we were able to get off. We met the ground crew at out planned evening stop near Vermillion, South Dakota, the Clay County

Recreational Area. Our evening program was not large, but we had a lot of interesting people with good questions. Frank got a white shirt, vest, and hat from me. He is going to try talking to students tomorrow. I hope things go well for him; he is really excited about it.

## Butch Bouvier
### *October 2001*

The "sandbar" incident stands out in Dale's comments as a sign of the crew beginning to learn their jobs. Please take note, when they grounded hard on a sandbar, there was no instant decision to "go over the side" to free *Raycliff*. Good ol' common sense again; no "mass exodus" over the side to free her, no immediate danger, so no hurry. My crew was beginning to learn the art of reading the situation and the urgency of it. This skill would save their bacon later in the voyage.

## Butch Bouvier
### *2013*

I fondly remember Terry as a likable guy—quiet and very thoughtful. I have always felt bad about this camera incident, as it was a brand-new digital type. Twelve years ago that was new technology, and they weren't cheap!

## Gary
### *Wednesday, October 3, 2001*

This was supposed to be the most difficult day on the river. We had only one teaching stop: at our evening layover near Vermillion, South Dakota. The day started off fresh and a little bit crisp. We had a nice, hot breakfast and just kind of lollygagged around for a bit. Tim's brother, Pat, was there and must have shot three or four rolls of film. He really seems like a nice guy. He always has a big friendly smile and a sparkle in his eye.

We started out under manpower; then, once we were basically out of camera range, we switched over to the towboat, as we had a lot of ground (water) to cover. And after yesterday's run, we didn't feel like a repeat performance. The day turned out to be a total joy, and was without incident.

Not far from the dock, we saw our one and only deer, a doe working her way upstream on the South Dakota side. She never got excited or bolted from our view. She just walked calmly up the bank and disappeared over a little mound into some sumac. It really amazed me that, with all the cover we saw and all the habitat available, the game was really pretty scarce.

As we proceeded downriver, we decided to make a little smoke. We got our rifles and started to take pot shots at twigs in the water, branches, and logs onshore. It's a good thing that supper did not depend on us, as it would have been a bit skimpy. Tim had a black powder six-shooter, and it was a lot of fun to shoot. You could actually see the ball travel to the target (or at least near it) most the time.

**This part of the trip had some of the prettiest scenery; some fantastic bluffs came right to the water's edge.** You could picture the Corps of Discovery moving away from the banks as they were caving off and crashing into the water. We fired the cannon several times in this area to hear the echo created between the bluffs. During this, we did flush out a flock  of turkeys. They didn't seem all that impressed with us; they simply jumped a small ditch and headed back from whence they came. At about this same time, a professional photographer came alongside and wanted to get some shots, so we shipped the oars and rowed downstream. Ann whipped out her GPS unit and figured that we were making around ten miles per hour. We all felt good about this until one of the guys pointed out that the Corps of Discovery sometimes covered eighty miles in a day on the way home in 1806.

The further downstream we went, the more spectators we met. We had one guy with a pirate flag go around us three or four times in less than a mile. We fired our cannon just to show him that we appreciated the company. A little while later we saw the same boat pulled up along a steep bluff. We didn't know what he was doing, but then he tossed a sparking cylinder into the water. We were trying to figure out just what was going on when it exploded with a great roar and a geyser of water maybe three feet high. I bet it doesn't take long to get your limit of fish when you're fishing with explosives! A little later we stopped on the bank to eat our sack lunches, which the ground crew had put together for us. We were amazed at the amount of damage the beavers were doing in this area. Trees of all sizes were cut down or girdled all the way around. Many of the trees had been felled into the river, and many more were bellied onto the shore. What surprised me the most was the size of the chips these toothy critters could cut in a bit. I would have thought that the pieces would be little slivers, but instead most were larger than a silver dollar.

As the days passed, it seemed as though the river taught us each a little more about itself. In doing so, it also taught us more about handling the boat. I watched this group of men and boys start to pull together and work as a team, and we did so without the military discipline that the Corps was subjected too. I could see how the Corps became a tight-knit group with each man knowing the other well enough to recognize his outline on a dark night. In the little bit of research I have done, it is interesting to see whom the captains chose to go on side trips or special assignments. After our shore lunch, we put back into the water and headed for our evening stop at Vermillion. The scenery started to change; the bluffs no longer crowded the banks, and the shore became more like what I had pictured for South Dakota. The land seemed more flat and arid. The trees gave way to pastureland or small patches of farmland, much like the Platte River in central Nebraska.

The day was spectacularly clear, and it got warmer as we went on. We came to an area that seemed to be in the middle of nowhere. There were nice little fishing cottages lining the Nebraska side of the river. The further we went, the bigger and nicer the cottages became. We didn't know if the ground crew was going to try to meet up with us along the way, or just meet us in Vermillion. We were getting hot and tired, so we decided to pull into a dock where there were some folks and take a break. The current in front of the dock was pretty strong. We manned the oars and started to back paddle to slow ourselves down. It's a good thing we were all up and working the oars, as Willard decided to take a shortcut to shore and turned right in front to us. We darned near ran him over. And if we had, I'm confident we would have deep-sixed him right then and there! Anyway, we missed him and made our way back upstream a short distance to the dock with no further problems.

Everyone except Willard, Terry, and myself went to a local bar for some liquid refreshments. We found a pump, and the local folks told us it was good water from a sand point. We tried it, and it was the coolest, sweetest water we had on the whole trip. While we waited for the crew to return, I lay down on the dock and dunked my head in the river, and it felt fantastic. We talked some more with the locals, and a really nice older couple wanted to know if we had enough room for a couple of stowaways. We ended up giving them a ride around the next bend in the river and dropped them off at their own dock. They seemed to enjoy their trip, and we sure enjoyed the short time we spent with them. After we dropped them off, it didn't seem like much longer until we came to our camping area just outside Vermillion. It was quite a ways from town, and we had arrived early, which allowed us ample time to set up camp and prepare for our presentations.

As the people came out, the sun was going down, and Butch had arranged for a generator and floodlights. The boat really looked sharp that night. Everyone seemed well pleased with the presentations, and of course they all enjoyed when Larry would shoot the cannon and I returned fire with my .58 caliber. One of the guys had Larry and Mike shoot the cannon after dark so he could photograph the flames barking out its mouth. That evening we made and enjoyed a large bonfire. It also turned out to be the coldest night of the trip so far. We put our little propane heater in our borrowed pyramid tent in the hopes that it would keep us warm. It wasn't long until it was nice and toasty in there; in fact, I slept in my shirt all night and stayed very comfortable. We decided to purchase a pyramid for ourselves when we got back for our future "skinner" outings. I am writing this part of the journals by candlelight, and this gives a whole new perspective to the process.

## Butch Bouvier
### October 2001

Gary's perspectives are always insightful and positive. As the person who put this whole thing together, I was very pleased to see a good and appreciative attitude. I had secretly hoped that some of the guys on the trip would start to really get into it and begin to identify with the members of the 1804–1806 expedition. Gary was not the only one who began to feel historically nostalgic about what we were doing, but he seemed to describe it best.

## Butch Bouvier
### 2013

This day went off without a hitch. The boat crew had a great time, and my ground crew was really coming together. I was a happy camper, to be sure!

## Tim
### Wednesday, October 3, 2001

The next morning broke clear and bright, and the wind had abated somewhat. My brother from Vermillion arrived and shot a lot of video that morning. We were able to take our time this morning, as we did not have any deadlines to meet and simply had to navigate down to Vermillion in a reasonable amount of time. Iowa Senator Steve joined us, and as we pushed off, we were anticipating a good run. As we maneuvered downstream, I tried to use landmarks, much like Lewis and Clark had, to determine distance covered. **After a couple of miles, though, we pulled out our firearms and began to target practice.** I had my .50 cal. and so lost track of my mileage estimations.

I noticed when I shot my gun that it didn't seem to have the power or range that it should. Larry, who was next to me, said that he noticed powder blowing into his face from my muzzle blast. He asked me how much charge I was putting in, and that was when I discovered that I was only charging my rifle with about forty-five grams of powder, whereas he was using close to one hundred grams of powder. I realized that I had set my charge measure for my naval pistol, which takes a substantially lower charge. Larry had proved once again that he was a weapons and armament expert. I did bring out my naval black powder six-shooter, which we had some fun with. I picked out a pair of badger holes about six feet apart on the bank about one hundred yards away and began firing, trying to hit between them. With the bank consisting of sand, we were able to see each shot land. Some were high and some were low, but with the very last shot, I was dead on target, for which I was rewarded with a lusty cheer from my shipmates.

Larry did have one problem with his armament. He did not have a proper ramrod for our bow cannon and was forced to use a smaller one from his portable cannon, which the ground crew played with. This caused him to frequently get his fingers pinched while ramming home the charge. It takes considerable force to pack the powder tight enough for a loud retort. His wasn't the only injury; with rough wood or sharp knives, there were a few other cuts and bruises to attend to. Larry's wife, Carolyn, was kept busy as our first-aid nurse.

We had packed lunch for Wednesday's journey, as we would not see the ground crew until evening when we landed. We decided that it would be fun to tie up and have a shore lunch, which we did and enjoyed it very much. There is something magical to me about being on the side of the river or in the middle of a sandbar that makes you feel like the river is all your own. After lunch we again cast our lot with the mighty Missouri and headed downstream. We soon came to the divided river around the three-mile island, which sat in the middle of the river. We headed for the South Dakota side, as I knew the Vermillion landing would be just around the bend. With the appearance of cabins along the South Dakota side, we knew we were getting close. And sure enough, a report from the shore crew cannon hailed our arrival. We were all a little concerned, as the current was very swift, and if we missed the landing it would be a tough row back. As we approached the cove, we tossed Butch our rope. He locked it down and swung us right into the cove like he had done it a hundred times before.

A lot of people from town came out to see us. They wanted to get on-board and get a feel for the pirogue. We built a huge bonfire, which played like a beacon on the far shore. The local fire department provided a trail-er-mounted generator and lighting system, which allowed folks to view the boat well into the evening. **A gentleman named Casey came down to the ramp in his wheelchair-equipped van, and we were able to assist him in**

**getting down to the boat dock and onto the bow of the boat.** He proved to have some knowledge of the river from this point downstream, as he had floated it many times in inner tubes. After some discussion, he agreed to provide guide service from here down to Rosenbaum Landing the next day. We were finally left to our own devices as the visitors thinned out and left. The breeze continued through the night, and you could feel a change in the weather.

## Butch Bouvier

### *October 2001*

I was up early with Dale to cook breakfast on this morning. As we got to the shelter where all of the cooking stuff was, I noticed a guy sacked out in a sleeping bag on one of the picnic tables. When we accidentally made enough noise to wake him, we were surprised to see Senator Steve. He had said he would hook up with us here, but you know how that goes with a busy politician. He kept his word, and he showed up; I like that!

I did lie about the *accidental* noise in the paragraph above. But I didn't know if we had a homeless guy, a fugitive from justice, or a dead body on that table, so I dropped a fry pan on the concrete. Up popped a state senator, so we got him a cup of coffee ASAP!

It was nice to get a visit from Casey. If you remember, Mike and I had met Casey in Vermillion the day we cooked up this trip. He had expressed an interest in what we were planning and asked if I would keep him up to date on our progress. I did, and here he was!

## Butch Bouvier
### 2013

Good memories!

# Day Six: A Historic Day

## Dale
### Thursday, October 4, 2001

Rainy and overcast all day. This was the poorest day we had since we left. I woke up early when it started to rain, and then dozed off again. I had the tailgate curtain down and was watching for Butch to light the lanterns and start the stoves. But Butch overslept too, so we were a little late getting breakfast started. The boat still made it off on time, though, so I took a few minutes and drove into Vermillion to make a couple of calls back to my office. We drove to Elk Point, South Dakota, and split up. The ground crew hung out while Frank, Butch, and I went to the local school to see if they wanted to brave the weather or do the program at the school. The principal checked the radar on his computer and decided that we would have a two-hour window so we could do the programs in the field as planned, and he turned out to be right! We had a good group of very interesting students. The town of Elk Point has a great deal of Lewis and Clark history. This is the where Patrick Gass was elected to replace Sgt. Floyd, who had died a few days before at present-day Sioux City. Nearly all the students knew some Lewis and Clark history. This was a large group of kids. **The small cove at Elk Point had a very tricky en-**

**trance, but our boat crew made it on the first try with Butch's expert help.** When they left Elk Point, they had to go back up the river to Ponca State Park. I didn't have anyone to drive my pickup, so I did not go with the pirogue. The story that was told

about this trip was that they were having great difficulty going upstream. A man from the park showed up with his powerful boat and attempted to tow the crew to safety, but he struck something with his out drive and drifted away. So they decided to cordelle. Upon my arrival at Ponca, I began searching downstream for some sight of the boat. When I saw them for the first time, there were three men onshore, cordelling it upstream. When Butch saw this, I thought he was going to do cartwheels! This was the first time this had been done for real in the last 150 years. We were writing a new chapter in the history book. We are now one team, working for the same goal! We camped at Ponca State Park, and Butch rented some cabins for us. I slept in my tin tepee, but did get a bath for the first time since Sunday.

## Butch Bouvier
### October 2001

Snatching the rope and swinging this boat and its crew into this inlet was pretty tricky, and I would have only one shot at it. I had to catch the rope, half roll it around a tree trunk, and pay it out as needed to allow the downstream momentum of the boat to carry it into the small harbor mouth. I got lucky, and she swung in like I actually did understand the physics of it.

Dale regrets missing this part of the journey as I did. It was historic, it did make me proud, but it also scared me half to death. The *Raycliff* was in trouble, and my wife was among the folks onboard, as well as a state senator. To say I was concerned would be an understatement.

## Butch Bouvier
### 2013

Mike Butler attained his personal best as a captain this day. He made the decision to cordelle, which saved the day.

## Bill
### Thursday, October 4, 2001

I arrived at Elk Point around 2:15 p.m., in plenty of time to catch the crew and boat before they departed for the afternoon to Ponca State Park. Much to all of our surprise, we had already passed the park in the morning, and we were now about three to four miles upstream. It was a struggle against the strong current (approximately seven miles per hour). Finally a park ranger came along and hooked onto us

with a powerful boat. The next one mile went along well, but then he hit something with his lower unit, and we immediately began to lose the ground we had just made. The oars were not up to the task, and we were drifting in a very strong current, virtually out of control, with a stone jetty in our path. Our salvation came from two hundred years back, when Captain Mike realized it was time for immediate action. He gave the command, "Cordelle! Cordellers ashore!... Rig a line!" Several of the younger and stronger crewmembers immediately jumped over the side and made their way to shore, while Cathy Bouvier and Senator Steve rigged a cordelle line high on the mast, as they instinctively knew they had to clear the debris along the

shore. Within minutes a full-size pirogue, the *Raycliff*, was under a full cordelle for real serious business up the mighty Missouri for the first time in probably more than 150 years!

I stayed onboard and offered any other assistance I could. Robbie and Nate rigged a second line to help cordelle. Cathy knew it was rigged wrong but only told me. There were numerous obstacles along the way, and this slowed down progress, but we were underway upstream against a strong current with a forty-two-foot boat weighing in excess of seven thousand pounds. Robbie and Nate eventually gave up their line, as it didn't seem to be helping much. The others continued all the way to Ponca and were exhausted, as it was no easy task! My arms were sore for several days afterward from the aggressive rowing with that large oar. The cordelle was indeed something to experience. It is quite possible that our crewmembers are the only people alive in the world to have accomplished it for real, with a real pirogue, on a real river—the mighty Missouri!

Once docked, we went immediately to dinner while Butch educated an interested public and secured the boat for us. Cabins were obtained for the evening for those who wanted one. Senator Steve, Terry, Tim, and I all chose to set up our tents right along the river's edge near the pirogue. We pitched our camp by flashlight in the dark and settled in for what was to be the coldest night we had yet to experience. Nevertheless, it was a peaceful and quiet evening, except for the snoring (I don't know about Tim).

This day was unique as it was the closest we would come to experiencing what the original expedition members did on their journey of discovery while working their way up the Missouri in 1804. I don't know how they made it without massive desertions, mutiny, or just plain giving up! That crew must have understood the importance of their undertaking.

## Butch Bouvier
### October 2001

Catherine confided in me recently that she instinctively knew how to rig a cordelle line just from watching me over the years. Mike Butler made the right call to send cordellers ashore. This was an emergency situation; the boat and her crew were in imminent danger, and they all realized that the only way to save the day was to get wet. I believe that even though Mike Butler made the right call, and the guys who went over the side to get to shore never hesitated, the real heroes of the day were Steve and my wife, Catherine. If Cathy and Steve had not rigged that cordelle line properly, all the rest would have been for naught.

I was at the dock in Ponca getting reports from the park rangers via radios. What I was hearing was not good, and I was getting very concerned. Finally I saw a masthead just behind an island about a mile downstream. Then I saw a cloud of smoke, and a few seconds later heard a loud report from the old girl's bow cannon. I knew then that my crew had pulled it off and were safely bringing her into dock.

I didn't see how until they were closer, but what a thrill to see a full cordelle on the old Missouri with an authentic nineteenth-century craft for the first time in possibly a hundred years or so. When I finally got the rest of the story, how Mike made the call, and the crew responded, I was very pleased. But when I heard how Catherine and Steve had rigged that cordelle line in a matter of minutes, I was so damn proud I could burst!

## Butch Bouvier
### 2013

Ditto!

## Gary
### Thursday October 4, 2001

This day started out cold and damp with a few sprinkles thrown in for good measure. Dale and I were the first ones up, and Dale started putting our meal together. People rolled out of their tents, etc. pretty much on their own this morning, with the exception of maybe Nate, who seemed to be a little the worse for wear, and this was due to a little bit of overindulgence. Anyway, we bundled up and found what protection we could from the rain. It turned out to be cold and clammy all day, with intermittent showers. After shoving off, some of the crew found warmth and shelter up under the bow and stern decks for temporary breaks from the weather. Often the guys would stomp their feet on the decks to shake a little water down on the "slackers" in what we called the **"rat holes."** They did offer the folks beneath them some coffee, though, but then would dribble it between the cracks in the deck just to be ornery. It was all in good fun, and no one got upset. Soon our guide was con-

cerned about some snags on our starboard side, so we headed across the river to avoid them, and we were hard aground within minutes. This turned out to be our most difficult grounding of the day. We put men into the water, some to find deep water and some to push. The rest

of us used push-poles. In general, we would free the stem, and then the bow would snag up, and vice versa. We were surprised when we finally cleared the bar and were on our way again. This part of the river was fairly wide and shallow, and the channel ran back and forth from side to side. You really had to stay on your toes and "read" the river.

Not long after the sandbar experience, we came upon some bridge construction that did not give us much room to maneuver. While Willard was pulling us toward the Nebraska side, we decided to give the working bridge crew a little treat, so we touched of the cannon. Some of them jumped, and one of them even looked like he hit the deck. Anyway, Willard got us through with flying colors. Our guide told us that this would be our chance to "shoot some rapids." We were coming up on an old diversion dam, which caused the river to drop about six feet in approximately twenty yards. In that large boat we hardly noticed it.

Not much further downstream, we came to a huge island that sat smack in the middle of the river. Our guide wasn't sure which side to take, so we sent Willard ahead to survey both channels. We dropped our anchor, but it did little more than slow us down. The current was very swift here, and we were drug down the channel with the flowing water. That current had the boat sideways and backwards, and we were out of control for a short time before Willard caught up with us and hooked on to get us straightened out.

The next few miles were pretty uneventful, other than watching large numbers of geese flying. It was still cold and dreary, but the worst of the rain was behind us for the day. It was and still is very difficult to estimate distance on the river. When I say, "It was only a little ways," this is only a very poor guess. It is amazing to me that Captain Clark was so accurate in his mileage. I would guess that he might have had some type of math equation to help him out. Then again, he may have been one of those guys like my grandfather who could simply eyeball something and be correct. Anyway, it didn't seem long after the island experience when we spotted the water tower at Elk Point. Mike remembered that our next stop was downstream from Elk Point proper, but before Ponca  Mike and Butch had scouted the route by car the month before, and now Mike was trying to get his bearings from the river. We had gone maybe a mile past town when all kind of sirens started blowing. We weren't sure what it was all about, but the thought that maybe we had gone past our stop did occur to us. As we went on down the river, we came to Ponca State Park. We knew that this was to be our nighttime stop and we were supposed to be at Elk Point first. So we turned the boat around and headed back upriver. Since we couldn't really communicate with the ground crew, we were pretty much winging it. Either Senator Steve or Tim used a cell phone to get in touch with the ground crew. It was determined that the spot we wanted was three or four miles downstream from a pipeline that bridged the river. We had seen this pipeline just past the park—and just before we had turned around. We decided to follow our new information and head back downstream. We were maybe a mile past the pipeline when we ran into a couple we recognized from a previous encounter and asked them the way to Rosenbaum Landing. One pointed downstream and one pointed upstream, and for some reason we turned the boat around again. After a short distance, and after much discussion, we decided to turn back downstream. After about three miles, we spotted the ground crew's flare and heard the report of the cannon.

After landing, we found that the ground crew had things all set up, and school kids had drinks and sandwiches ready for us. One young lady did a double take when I asked her for a dog-meat sandwich. The young man working with her didn't even bat an eye when he said, "I'm sorry, sir, but we only have ham. We were getting ready to butcher the dog when the pig ate it." We all had a good chuckle. Tim's wife met him here, as he had to leave the group for a business meeting.

After the programs, we put back in and headed upstream for Ponca. This part of the river has begun to channelize itself, and it was deep and swift. We made the turn upstream, and with Willard's boat wide open and us rowing for all we were worth, we traveled maybe fifteen feet in fifteen minutes. We moved closer to shore, trying to find less swift water, and made a little better headway. Ann checked her GPS unit and informed us that we were making about one-tenth of a mile per hour. We knew we were in deep trouble at this point; Ponca was still four miles ahead, and it was getting late in the afternoon. We did not want to be on the river in this current after dark! Within about one mile of our previous landing, and about the time we felt we could row no more, a Department of Natural Resources ranger from Ponca State Park showed up with a powerful boat and took us under tow.

We had not traveled more than half a mile when his motor conked out and left us drifting toward a dangerous wing dam. Mike and I discussed the problem briefly and decided to try a cordelle line. We moved closer to shore and sent men over the side with a line. Butch's wife, Catherine, and Steve rigged the line to the mast, and we went into a full cordelle! It worked beautifully, and we made steady progress upstream. Willard tried to assist with his small boat and motor, and he struck bottom with his prop. This was the first time I saw Willard get upset during the trip, which is amazing considering the amount of crap we gave him! Nathan served as "trailbreaker," kicking down brush and breaking off limbs for the cordelle crew. I tried to hold the boat as close to shore as possible, but I had to avoid some huge snags and deadfalls at some points. This maneuvering caused the ground cordelle crew to have to climb over obstacles and pass the rope from one to another. Meanwhile Catherine and Steve were whipping the rope up to get it over these obstacles. We finally spotted our landing at Ponca, so Catherine and Steve loaded the cannon and touched it off to let them know we were coming.

In all the excitement and genuine concern for our safety, and the safety of the boat, we didn't realize until after we had tied up that we were probably the first people to perform this maneuver in more than a hundred years. Butch and the rest of the ground crew were so excited at the sight of a full cordelle that they could hardly speak. They just screamed hysterically and cheered us on. I'd swear Butch had tears in his eyes.

That evening we feasted on a wonderful roast beef dinner. Butch sprang for some cabins for "his crew," and my family and I shared one with Buffalo "Bill" Sanders. I still want to get a T-shirt that says, "I slept with Buffalo Bill."

## Butch Bouvier
### October 2001

With all the other excitement of the day, I was glad that Gary shared the details of the bridge and its challenges, as well as the indecision about where the next stop was. I had screwed this up and hoped that I could correct it for the safety of my crew. Unknown to them, I was frantically lining up the Nebraska Department of Natural Resources towboat to help them get back upstream to Ponca. I knew for a fact that Willard's boat could not accomplish it, and they could not row it before dark. With confirmation that the Department of Natural Resources boat would hook up with them, I thought it would be safe to ask Catherine if she would like to join the boat crew for this part of the trip. She eagerly jumped at the chance. Little did I know that I was putting her, the rest of the crew, and the boat in harm's way—through which she and everyone else aboard would shine like a new penny!

## Butch Bouvier

### 2013

I was recently asked to bring another one of my boats to Ponca for a major event. I elected to not launch it there, as the water is very swift, and the channels are small. I had to learn this the hard way twelve years earlier.

## Tim

### Thursday, October 4, 2001

About the same time I heard voices in camp, the first raindrops started hitting my tent. Today would be another early-start day with an appointment at Rosenbaum Landing near Elk Point, South Dakota, with an estimated three hundred kids from local schools. I broke camp as quickly as I could, trying to keep from getting my gear wet, but was only partially successful. We had a quick and delicious omelet made in a Dutch oven for breakfast before it was time to set off for what was to be the wildest day yet. We needed to get immediately to the Nebraska side of the river from our landing. To get there we had to go almost due south, directly across the current, to a large section of "cut bank," and then turn immediately due east to stay in the main channel. Since I was somewhat familiar with this part of the river, I went with Willard in the chase boat, while Casey in his wheelchair rode the bow deck and helped guide us. We made the first crossing OK, but when we tried to cut back east, we ran hard aground on a large and wide sandbar. Willard and I let loose the towrope, as we could be of no assistance in this shallow of water (approximately six inches). I had worn swim trunks under my jeans in anticipation of a possible shallow-water rescue. I shucked my jeans and climbed out and pushed Willard back into deeper water. I then returned to the pirogue, and Doc, Terry, and I tried to locate some deep water so we could direct the crew which way to work the boat. With us pulling ropes, others pushing and rocking, and the onboard crew using setting poles, we were able to move her off. To my surprise, we even pushed a ridge in the sand, which was nearly at the level of the water.

Our next encounter was with the new Vermillion/Newcastle Bridge still under construction at this time. We saluted the bridge crew with our cannon, and they stopped work to see this once-in-a-lifetime vision of the white pirogue floating down the river below them. Downstream of the bridge about six hundred yards was an area where the water appeared turbulent and choppy and gave the appearance of being shallow. Casey was familiar with this and signaled for us to shoot right through it, which we did quite successfully. A couple more miles downstream, we came across the mouth of the James River, and it was obvious this was an embarkation point for small pleasure craft; it was almost like a small marina. I spared Willard at the steering for a while and learned firsthand what it was like to tow a seven-thousand-pound boat with a fifteen-horsepower motor. The minute the keels of both craft were not lined up, the momentum of the pirogue could be felt on the small rowboat, and it was very difficult to maintain control. The helmsman had to make corrections instantaneously to stay the course in order to effect corrections on the pirogue.

I had felt a little sorry for Willard and Terry, who had been forced to spend all day on the small chase boat. During my time on the chase boat, I missed the camaraderie of the pirogue crew, but with Willard I felt a sense of adventure, which for me had permeated the whole trip. This trip was turning out to be something much larger than just a float trip down the river, which is what I had signed on for. My time with Willard allowed me to become better acquainted with him and better understand the tremendous contribution he had made to the adventure.

I have spent hours on the Missouri, both duck hunting and fishing, in the summer, fall, and even the winter. I've been on the river when it was below zero and snowing, and back up the chutes at Springfield at night when the only thing we could see was what our searchlight illuminated. With all that said, I still feel that I learned more about river navigation on this trip than I had ever learned before. I learned that snags sticking up normally indicate deeper water and faster current; a log lying horizontally indicates the edge of the channel; a fresh-cut bank indicates a strong current and deep water; and an old-cut bank indicates a change in the main channel, which will leave you hung up on a bar.

I was keeping my eyes peeled for Rosenbaum Landing, as I had never been there before and wasn't sure where it was. I was sure it was on the South Dakota side, as we were to give programs to kids from the Elk Point school system. I saw the old bridge pilings opposite Ponca State Park and was sure we had passed the noon program landing. Since I knew that we were to make camp that evening at Ponca, and I was sure we were not going to try to make a long run upstream late in the day, we turned around and headed slowly back upstream. But then we changed our minds and headed back downstream. We came across an older couple and asked directions. They were not sure, so we decided to turn back upstream. But the going was too rough, and we once again headed back down, hoping for the best. Before long we heard the report of the ground crew's cannon, and we were much relieved to know we were heading the right direction. I was amazed to realize that the plan was to have evening camp over four miles upstream from our noon program with the river as deep and swift as it was in this area.

Once again the landing was a little tricky, but our Butch handled the ropes we threw him expertly, and we swung right into the small inlet. Willard had killed his motor after striking some debris, and we darned near ran him over again. Coffee and hot sandwiches were provided, and after the cold, damp day, they were very welcome. Also welcome was the sight of my wife Debbie, whom I hadn't seen since Saturday morning. This was my vacation but not necessarily hers. I had to say good-bye to my new friends, as I had some business to attend to the next day. I will continue to look forward to the Bicentennial of the Lewis and Clark Expedition with even more appreciation now. The celebration will engage tourists with the history of the expedition, which provided sound knowledge of the western United States. The bicentennial will mark the anniversary of when the people of this new nation grew to understand that their country would stand united and spread from sea to shining sea for the next two hundred years! Special thanks to Butch and Catherine Bouvier for dreaming this trip up, funding it, and treating us to the adventure of a lifetime!

## Butch Bouvier
### October 2001

Tim had been a valued member of the crew, and we would miss him. I heard later that when he was told the story of the cordelle to Ponca, he almost cried. He had experienced so much from something that he thought would just be a simple downriver trip. I hope that everyone got as much from it as he did.

## Butch Bouvier
### 2013

I still wish that Tim could have had that last great experience cordelling; he had earned it!

# Day Seven: Our Last Day

## Dale

### Friday, October 5, 2001

We were up early and had pancakes for breakfast. This was the coldest morning we have had, but it cleared off and was a mild day. Frank came to me this morning, and I gave him the white pants that I had to complete his uniform. He is now fully outfitted in an authentic Lewis and Clark Expedition uniform. I rode the pirogue down to the Adams Homestead stop for our noon programs. The boat arrived a little before all the ground crew had, which turned out to be fortunate for us, as it allowed us time to get set up for the three-hundred-plus students who swarmed down on us. This was our largest program yet, complete with a lot of media coverage. As with our previous stops, I believe that we left the students all wanting more information. It is my hope that we sparked enough interest in them that they will go back and do their own research.

We left the homestead with the wind at our backs for a fun ride to our final destination, the marina in South Sioux City. **The wind was stiff, and we attained a downstream speed of over twelve miles per hour and rising, until we lost our nerve and reefed the main.** As we got closer to Sioux City, we entered the part of the river the Corps of Engineers had reworked and channeled. We got caught behind a rock jetty. This is a very dangerous place to be in an unpowered boat! Instinctively, the men on the port side rowed, while the men on the starboard side pushed off, and we cleared the jetty without even scratching the paint. At this point, I knew that we could go right on downstream to Saint Louis, no problem! We were a team! But in less than an hour, we would be tying up for the last time, at least for this year.

The adventure of adventures was over for now. As we sat at the bar in the hotel, Butch was already making plans for next year. Back in my room after a hot bath, I was lying in bed with a TV and a remote. I picked up the remote to catch up on the world I had left a week ago, but thought better of it and decided to not to go back to the real world until the next morning. It had been a wonderful week! I thought about the wagon trains that I had been on and the other river experiences that I had, and the dozens of reenactment camps. Nothing compared to this. This was a real-life learning and living experience. I will relive it over and over for the rest of my life, and I'll take this wonderful time to the grave with me. Thanks, Butch!

## Butch Bouvier
### *October 2001*

Once again my bride stood tall on this adventure; quite a feat for someone who is vertically challenged! There were so many kids and so little time, she just instinctively took charge and started putting them in groups that we could handle. **I worked right alongside her, and when the kids left, we both just collapsed on a park bench.** Everyone did a great job with programming the events, though most had not really done much of it, or in many cases none at all. I would have to vote as our most improved programmer: Frank Koeppe and his alter ego Cpl. Richard Worfington.

## Butch Bouvier
### *2013*

Adams Homestead still holds the record for number of students attending programs in one session for my crew.

## Bill

### *Friday, October 5, 2001*

Cool, breezy, but sunny. A few people hadn't boarded the boat yet, and it was obvious that we were going to be short drivers, so I volunteered to drive a vehicle to Adams Homestead. It was a nice, warm job, but I was anxious to get back onboard in the afternoon. The midafternoon program at Adams turned out to be our largest of the trip. My estimate is over three hundred kids. I boarded when the boat shoved off, and the trip to Sioux City was great. We had a fabulous tail wind, and with all sail unfurled, we were making over nine knots. One mile from dock, my favorite hat blew off and sank right to the bottom. As we approached the dock, Larry fired the cannon as fast as he could reload it, and Gary was firing his .50 caliber rifle in between Larry's reports—it was great.

A nice crowd awaited us (another senator, the mayors of Sioux City and South Sioux City, and Department of Natural Resources officials). **Butch spoke to the group, explaining his goals for this trip and how his business had bankrolled whatever part of the trip was not covered by donations (this turned out to be a couple thousand).**  Speaking of donations, I presented Lora Butler, the treasurer for the group, a check from my company for $2,000. We had a nice program at the Sergeant Floyd Monument with a dinner back at the park afterwards. I want to give special thanks to the following people…Butch Bouvier, boatbuilder and dreamer; Butch's wife, Cathy, who is his anchor to reality; Mike Butler, captain of the boat; the crew of the boat; and the ground crew.

The moment I stepped off the boat for the last time, I felt a sense of sadness, as if I was leaving an old friend behind. I also felt a sense of pride and appreciation for being allowed this brief look into the lives of the crew of the

Corps of Discovery—and thankfulness for what they endured to open up this river and this region of our country.

As a result of this trip, I will feel a closer attraction to the river for the rest of my life.

## Butch Bouvier
### October 2001

Ground me in reality? That's no fun. Don't want to do that!

## Butch Bouvier
### 2013

Reality? Never!

## Gary
### Friday, October 5, 2001

Friday morning, the last day of the journey. I got up fairly early and thought I might be running a little late. Bill had already gone, and I had not heard him leave. I got dressed and walked over to the shelter house. Bill and Butch were working on getting a fire cranked up in the fireplace. My feelings were mixed. I was looking forward to the time on the river, and yet I knew this was the last day of our journey. It had been so much fun, I did not want it to end. After breakfast we headed on down to the boat to load up and head downstream. There were people waiting there to see us off. The day turned out pretty nice, with sun and a following wind. We sailed all day, and at times we created a wake at the bow of the boat.

When we arrived at Adams Homestead, Dale and Becky were waiting for us, along with Terry. The rest of the group was at the visitor center having lunch. The boat crew were to eat lunch next, but as luck would have it, the kids started showing up, so Dale and Becky started getting everything organized. Then Catherine showed up, and between the three of them, we got the show on the road. This session was wonderful because of the large numbers that showed up, but also difficult because of the shortened amount of time and the disparity in the ages of the kids. At times it seemed we would hardly get started with one group before it was time to rotate to the next station.

The last part of the river trip was interesting in that the closer we got to Sioux City, the fancier the houses became. Many of them had their own harbors carved out of the banks and lined with various kinds of river rock. We also found that by getting fairly close to the jetties, we could catch the current where it shot off the end, and this would increase our water speed. If we stayed too close to shore on the upriver side, the wind and current would try to pull us into the jetty. We did have a couple of close calls, and actually did kiss the rocks one time on the starboard side. As we got to the edge of town, Larry started to fire the cannon, and I started firing the .58. When we went under the bridge, I had a big charge in the rifle and touched it off. The thing just roared and echoed like a beast. It was a total hoot! The current was strong, and the opening to the marina was small, so our landing was not as graceful as we would have liked in front of the dignitaries. But with Butch's help once again, we made it with no one getting hurt.

At the landing in Sioux City, we were met by various dignitaries who gave different speeches about the river and promised to make our visitor center a reality. Bill (on behalf of his company) presented the group with a check for $2,000. We then loaded on a bus for a trip to the Sergeant Floyd monument, where Bev Hinds gave a presentation. **Probably one of the most moving parts of the journey was at the monument.** Doc dug out a plug of sod he had brought with him from Kentucky (the birthplace of Sergeant Floyd) and transplanted it at the monument, taking his new plug with him to plant in Kentucky. He also put a plug of tobacco on the monument, along with a pint of genuine Kentucky moonshine. **While he was doing this, a group of us gave a military salute**

with our black powder rifles, firing them past the monument in the direction of Kentucky. When this was over, Doc thanked us for our show of camaraderie. In looking around, I saw more than one eye with moisture in it.

The rest of the evening was pretty anticlimactic. We shared our last meal together and started to say our good-byes. We spent some time at the bar at the Marina Inn, swapping stories and making plans for the future. Some of the plans included getting together again. Hopefully we will do the trip again. I pray that we do and our talk is not just empty promises like so often happens.

## Butch Bouvier

### *October 2001*

The landing in Sioux City was as Gary described, not as graceful as some in the past. The boat was approaching at twice the speed it normally did. I was on a steep bank of boulders, and the nearest thing to tie off to was about fifteen feet up this bank. It was an old piling sticking up about eight feet. To complicate matters, the soonest the crew could throw me a rope was about thirty feet in front of this piling, as there was a large fence down to the water's edge, which the rope would not clear. The next problem was that the rope was soaking wet; I never did find out why. And there was an iron weight tied to the end of the rope, which for some unknown reason, my boat crew thought they needed in order to heave it to me. I had shared some concerns about this landing with the ground crew, so one of them decided to get a local volunteer to "help" me with it. This guy shadowed me as I worked my way around that fence as best I could. As the boat approached, Larry threw the line right at my head. The iron weight missed me by inches, and as I scrambled to grab up this wet line and turned to scramble up the hill to the old piling, I ran right over my helper! When I finally got to the piling, I had less than eight feet of line left, so I threw a clove hitch around that pole as quick as I could and prayed that the rope would hold—and that I could keep it from slipping. The crew had tied the rope to *Raycliff's* bow bitt, so when she came to the end of the line, she immediately began to swing around with her stern pointing downstream. I don't know how many pounds of pressure were on that 3/4-inch manila line, but when she finally came to rest, it was not only bone dry, but was closer to 1/2-inch thick! I just sat on the bank exhausted for a few minutes as the crew pulled her backwards and slipped her into the harbor.

The Triumphant Return of the White Pirogue was over. All were safe, and I hope well satisfied with the results. We held a brief ceremony at the Sergeant Floyd monument. Then Frank and I loaded *Raycliff* and headed for Lewis and Clark State Park.

## Butch Bouvier
### *2013*

Over, yes, but never forgotten.

# Chapter Four

# Outbound and Against the Current

With *Raycliff* safely home from her maiden voyage, I started thinking about another trip. This time I wanted to go upriver, from Fort Randall Dam to Pierre, South Dakota. I had concluded that we would definitely need some power for such a trip. So over the course of the winter, I punched a hole in *Raycliff's* bottom and installed a covered wet well. I was able to scrounge up a used forty-horsepower, temperamental, two-cycle outboard, which I installed, along with a hidden gas tank under the foredeck.

Very early the following spring, I received a call from some folks in Niobrara, Nebraska, which is about sixty miles upriver from Onawa. They remembered *Raycliff* and her crew, as we had stopped and programmed there the year before. They were to have a weekend event on the riverfront and wanted me to bring the boat back for programs and rides. We struck a deal. I invited a few of the original crew along, offering to cover their expenses, and we headed north. This was going to give me a great opportunity to try out the new motor and wet well installation on the river—a test run for our next voyage!

Frank Koeppe was unavailable for this trip, and Niobrara was not that far, so I decided to haul *Raycliff* up there behind my 1970 Ford truck. Now the boat and trailer together weigh about four and a half tons, so a three-quarter-ton pickup should be able to haul it, right? Let's just say it was an interesting trip! I took it very slow, and even made it past the weigh station with no trouble. (I haven't figured that one out yet, but we got there safely!) OK, maybe it wasn't *that* safe...but we did get there! Resolutions: 1) Do not *ever* try something like that again, and 2) Make sure Frank is available *before* scheduling any events with the *Raycliff*.

The weekend at Niobrara was very successful. **The new motor installation worked well, and everyone had a great time.** The last evening onsite, we were kicking back and winding down on the boat when this guy wandered down the path to our mooring site. I invited him aboard for some conversation and a glass of wine. **His name was Matt. He had recently retired from the US Army and was footloose and fancy-free.** He was a history buff, and though I didn't know it until he left the boat later that night, he would be the pilot for our upriver trip in the fall.

After a successful trial run, I knew that the *Raycliff* could revisit a portion of Lewis and Clark's outbound expedition—and journey against the current this time. So I started making plans over the next few weeks. The adventure was planned to start just above the Fort Randall Dam. We would then head upriver to Pierre en route for their Goose Festival to be held in the late fall.

While still in the planning stages for the trip, I ran into an old friend from my body shop days. I told him of the adventure we were planning. "Big John" (he's almost 7 feet tall) and I met back in the 1970s, when I did some body work on his 1956 Chevy Nomad. I had seen him only on occasion since the mid-1980s, but to my surprise he expressed an interest in joining us on the river. So I invited him along!

Now I had put together a small crew, and once again lined up my old buddy, Frank Koeppe, to haul the *Raycliff* to the launch site. I had invited several of my crew from the first trip to join us. I offered to provide their rooms at the Governor's Inn in Pierre, and we were to have another grand experience running the river and programming.

After Frank Koeppe and his wife, Vicki, delivered the *Raycliff,* they decided to hang out with us. (Actually, I think it was Frank's alter ego, Cpl. Worfington, who just could not allow them turn around and go home after delivering her.) And with Frank on the boat and Vicki driving the Big Green Machine from stop to stop, I'd have another crewmember onboard and an additional ground crew member. We were ready to begin our adventure.

We launched her at the first boat ramp we could find, and we traveled upriver about a mile to a small cove that was also accessible to vehicles so that Vicki could hook up with us. We beached the *Raycliff* just as Vicki was pulling in with the now-empty trailer. **We met some nice folks, fried some fish over our campfire,** and made plans for our early-morning departure.

While visiting around the campfire that evening, I spent some time cautioning Big John about the Missouri River and its ultimate goal, which is to kill you if you're stupid enough to give it a chance to! That muddy old girl has a few other tricks up her sleeve also. I remembered from our first trip, when we had beached the *Raycliff* just below the Fort Randal Dam spillway the night before, that the water level had fallen quite a bit overnight and caused us some difficulties. We discovered later that the water level went down because water wasn't being released through the generators due to a decreased demand for electricity. If you think about this, it all makes good sense. The more electricity is needed, the more water is required to make it. Never one to forget a lesson learned the hard way, now we were above the dam near the rear of the reservoir. We should be in good shape. So what do you think happened to the water level overnight when the generators need more water? Well, the water level dropped above the dam, and go figure, the locals had to run their air conditioners this particular night! In the morning we found our wonderful boat aground. Just goes to prove that you can never out-guess that ornery old river!

OK, so our early-morning departure was delayed, while we tried to get our five-thousand-pound boat off the beach. There was no moving it by hand, and it seemed our only option would be to wait until the water level rose again. Frank Koeppe and the Big Green Machine to the rescue! (If my memory serves me correctly, this was his idea until it went south, and then it was mine.) Well, maybe it *was* my idea, and I conned him into trying it. Picture this: The parking lot is about thirty-five feet from the water's edge, as the crow flies, and it's all sand and downhill to the river after that, so driving a vehicle down to the boat to push it off would just not work. But the Big Green Machine had a trailer in tow that was just about thirty-five feet long. Are you getting the picture yet?

With careful and deliberate precision (and several tries), Frank had the trailer backed down the embankment, about two feet from *Raycliff*'s bow. By this time, his rear tires were right at the edge of the soft sand, but we were so close. We were not going to quit now! Hell, we should be able to go just two more feet, wouldn't ya think? Frank gently eased the end of the trailer against the bow of our beached whale and gave her a good nudge. She slid right into the water. She was afloat and ready to go!

All we needed to do now was to get the Big Green Machine and the trailer off the hillside so we could load up and go. Frank expertly chose the lowest gear he had and very slowly revved the engine. And with the experience and precision from years of trucking, he instantly buried all eight rear tires up to the axle in sand.

We were standing around scratching our heads when this guy shows up in a pickup truck. We conned him into trying to help us out with his rear-wheel drive, six-cylinder truck. I often wonder why people do the things they do. We had no right to expect his 2,500-pound truck to move an 18,000-pound semitruck, with a 2,000-pound trailer attached to it, but we did, and he agreed to give it a try. Had we been young, good-looking girls, I could understand him agreeing to help, but we were bearded, middle-aged mountain-men types with huge knives strapped to our sides and black-powder weapons on hand. OK, maybe it was fear, but he was willing to help, at any rate. After breaking two small tow straps, and almost jerking his bumper off, we showed some mercy and thanked him for trying and sent him on his way.

Now we had to put on our thinking caps, if we were ever to get going. The *Raycliff* was ready, so we would not have to wait for the water to rise, but if we couldn't get this monster truck off this hillside, we were basically screwed. Personal note for future reference: Semitrucks are *not* off-road vehicles. Well, I never go anywhere without a pocketknife, and usually a jack of some kind. I had an old farm handyman, and Frank had a couple of hydraulics. We found some old scrap wood along the shore, built a base for the jacks, and got them under the truck frame. We then unhooked the trailer so it would slide off the fifth wheel when we got the truck moving. We jacked up both sides, found the top of an old picnic table, and got that under the tires. We finally got the Big Green Machine back on solid ground. Now with power and traction, we chained up the trailer, drug it up to solid ground, jacked it up, and re-hooked it to the truck. Then we just looked at each other and laughed our butts off! We also took that old picnic table top along, just in case. Three hours late, we pointed the *Raycliff* north up the muddy Missouri, while Vicki headed up the road to meet us at the first scheduled stop. This was quite an interesting start to yet another one of my crazy adventures.

With Matt at the tiller, me on that cranky old motor, Frank still a little uncomfortable so far from land, and Big John, we headed north, across Lake Francis Case behind Fort Randal Dam. I suggested to Matt that we stay about fifty feet off shore, just in case that cranky motor quit. The wind and waves began to increase, so I opened the old motor up a bit, to keep our progress and maintain some control. We knew this was to be about a fifteen-mile straight shot until we once again reached the moving waters of the muddy Missouri, so we settled in for an easy and relaxing boat ride.

## Knowledge Nook
### How rudders work and how to measure a boat's speed

*This is a good time to explain the action of a rudder on a boat. Some will think I'm insulting their intelligence to explain this, but trust me, it is not understood by everyone. A vast number of folks have never been at the tiller, steering gear, or outboard motor of a small boat. Those who have understand that it's different from an auto, as you are steering from the rear, rather than the front. They can pretty quickly grasp that the rudder works the same way, but with one major difference, i.e., you don't have to be moving with an outboard-equipped boat to turn her, as it is the thrust from the outboard providing the turning power. With boats equipped with rudders and a fixed-position motor, forward motion is mandatory to have any control of direction. The more control required, the more speed is necessary. Without the power of the water against the side of the rudder, you have no control over your direction. This makes slowly approaching a dock a very tricky maneuver.*

*With modern science, we have seen all kinds of mechanical objects to control rudder-equipped boats and ships at very slow speeds. It all started with tugboats and continues today. They are aided by side thrusters and engine pods below the ship, which can turn 360 degrees. These modern helps are usually relegated to large ships, tugboats, or fancy motor yachts.*

*Now, turn your mind to a river situation. If you sit and study workboats on a major river for a while, you will eventually realize that they seem to be moving a little faster downstream than upstream. The same amount of speed, through the water, required for control of barges upstream, is required for downstream. No more, no less. Fuel is money, and they want to be economical. The only difference is the speed of the river. Upriver travel is minus the river's speed, and downriver travel is plus the river's speed, generally speaking.*

*Now if you're watching boats on a river to confirm this, please ignore most of the small pleasure speedboats, as most of them go flat out all the time. Considering that almost all rivers have a fair share of debris floating down them, especially the Missouri and the Mississippi, this would seem an imprudent thing to do, in my opinion; but that's what they do.*

*In the early 1800s, when traveling downstream in one of these mackinaw boats, keelboats, or many other types of boats, which have the capability to* go both upstream and down, you had the same problem of slow speed or no speed control through the water. **The old-timers easily solved this problem with a U-joint of sorts. They lengthened the tiller arm and mounted it on a U-joint or gimbal at the stern of the boat, very near the balance point between the actual rudder and the end of the tiller arm.** This allowed the fellow in control to lift the rudder out of the water, swing it left or right, lower it into the water, and pull

left or right on the tiller, thus forcing the stern of the boat to move, and repeat as needed in a sweeping manner; thus moving the stern of the boat in the opposite direction. These were called steering oars, or sweeps. This can be done with the boat sitting still, if need be. Problem solved, 1800s style!

Here are a couple of interesting historical notes. **The Vikings had a "steering oar" at the right rear of their boats.** It was vertical and acted as a rudder, rather than a sweep. I mention it here because this is where we got the term "starboard" to refer to the right side of a boat or ship. "Steering board" simply shortened to "starboard." Another historical note: if you read the Lewis and Clark Expedition journals for the last month they were at Mandan, in the spring of 1805, you will find that one of the fellows was busy fitting the barge with a "steering oar" for its downstream

trip back to Saint Louis. These fellows understood the problems facing them!

*We know for a fact that the keelboat/barge had a rudder, with some sort of hinged rudder irons, at least two or more, and they only moved right or left. This would make it mandatory to have a sweep or a steering oar fitted for a downstream trip. In the journals, they talk about breaking the irons (notice the plural) of the rudder on the pirogues at least twice on the upstream trip. It's not one hundred percent certain, but I would bet that when the little white pirogue headed downstream, she was fitted in the same way.*

*As long as we are talking about Lewis and Clark, let me touch on this little tidbit, and you can decide what the facts are. I mentioned earlier about the speed of boats on the river. You have probably all heard about the speed of a ship on the ocean being measured in knots. Currently, there is some discussion whether this is a measure of speed or distance, but nonetheless, it is used. And I will explain why and how it works. As my kids used to say, "In the olden days," the speed of a ship at sea was determined using a special rope, an hour glass, or a clock and a piece of wood or cloth. The rope had knots tied in it at predetermined intervals.* **This rope, which was usually wound on a spool called a "reel," was attached to a flat piece of wood, often called a "log" or "chip," in such a manner that the piece would travel flat against the water, much like a kite flies flat against the wind.** *The log would be thrown overboard, and a sand-filled minute-glass would imme-*

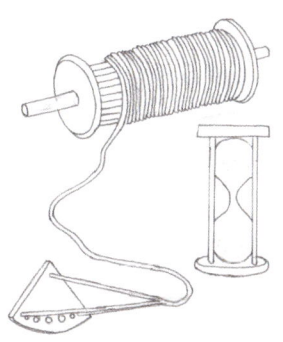

*diately be turned over, or the clock's second hand would be noted. As the rope was pulled through the hands of a seaman, the number of knots he passed in his hand over a given period of time would be counted. Now you can see where the term "knots" came from and how it worked. It's all done with modern equipment today, but is still called "knots." Once you know what the ship's speed through the water is, you can judge distance traveled by hours traveled, simple math. When navigating the oceans of the world, distance traveled is very critical to knowing where you are.*

*Now, just for fun and to make you think...*

*For our "Expedition Fact or Fiction," whichever you decide, picture this: Here you are, following my suggestion and sitting along the bank of the Muddy MO or Old Miss and probably enjoying the view immensely while noting boat speeds up and downstream. You are not determining their speed through the water, but rather it's speed judged by the static shoreline. Also remember this fact: the speed of a river will change with the changing of its width, especially in its turns. The water will run faster and deeper on the outside of the turn or bend and much shallower and slower on the inside. Many Lewis and Clark historians swear up and down that onboard the keelboat/barge, the captains had a log and reel for determining the speed of the boat. I don't believe that for a moment, as it would have only told them the speed of the boat through the water at a particular given moment and on that particular portion of the river. This information would be useless in determining river miles traveled. I don't believe they had a log and reel as part of their equipment, as I see no possible use for it. What do you think? Fact or fiction?*

## Now, where were we?

Oh, yes, on our "easy, relaxing" trip across Lake Francis Case. We were about fifty feet off the shoreline, and the wind was coming up. The lake started swelling in long twenty to thirty-foot swells, about one to one and a half feet from trough to peek. If you were prone to seasickness, you wouldn't have wanted to be aboard with us. Frank was getting nervous, as was Big John. Matt and I were concerned about that motor quitting, but other than that, having a ball.

I was on the foredeck, with the wind in my face, **listening to the *Raycliff* pound against the waves,** and mentally patting myself on the back for building such a sound craft, when something caught my eye. Out ahead, about eighty feet or so, I noticed something floating along in the waves.

The odd thing was that you could only see it in the troughs of the swells, and it disappeared when it hit the crest. It looked initially like a bunch of round, grayish-brown, kind-of rusty upside-down coffee cans, as strange as that sounds. These items intrigued me; what in the heck were they? And then I figured it out; they were upside-down or sealed metal cans of some sort. They were obviously waterlogged or filled with something, as they had very little positive buoyancy, which allowed them to bob up and down with the waves. When the wave crest hit them, there wasn't enough buoyancy left to keep them afloat—simple scientific deduction. Damn, I was proud of myself! Curious as to just what type of can they were, I instructed Matt to steer toward them, so that I could retrieve one and inspect it. As we got closer, something just didn't look right. I guided Matt a bit to port, so I could lean over the side and retrieve one as it passed by. Then what I saw horrified me. They were not cans at all, as I had smugly surmised; they were the tops of trees, which before the waters behind the dam had risen, had been sawn off, so they were now about two feet below the surface! We were smack-dab in the middle of a minefield of pilings, which could put a hole my girl in an instant. Have you ever seen a war movie where the soldiers wander into an enemy minefield, and all of a sudden someone yells, "Everyone freeze! We're in a minefield!"? Well, *we could not freeze!* Now the hollering part I had down pat, left…right…left, and Matt expertly followed my instructions as we wove our way into deeper water. We didn't tear the motor from its mount and didn't put a hole in the boat. We did scratch her paint a bit, but that just adds "character." As we hit deeper water and safety, I took a big breath of relief. As I looked back at Frank and Big John, I would describe the looks on their faces, but I'm not sure I could…or that I even should. It was either pure luck, my skill as a spotter, Matt's skill as a helmsman, or God who helped us out. We were not that good or lucky, so I have to say, thank you, Sir!

You might think that this first day on the river would just have to get better. Guess again. The wind got stronger, and the waves reached two to three feet, so we headed for shore, as the old girl couldn't take that for too much longer. Unfortunately, the shoreline was rocky, and if we beached her on those rocks, they would have beaten a hole in her bottom in minutes. So we hugged the shoreline again, hoping for no more trees, and straining our eyes for some sort of safe harbor. Finally, I spotted an opening to a small harbor. The entrance was narrow and strewn with round, bowling-ball-sized boulders. But if we could get her in there, we could weather the storm in relative safety, as once past the entrance, it was all sandy beach. But first we had to get through that entrance, and of course it had to be at right angles to the wind. I worked the motor controls while Matt manned the tiller, and we crabbed our way through the channel to safety. For those of you who may not know crabbing, it is when you point the boat at such an angle to the wind that she actually will travel a straight course. It's possible that you have seen small aircraft do this in a heavy wind.

Well, things were looking like we would make it, and we almost did. Just another twenty feet and we would be clear of the rocks, when the motor coughed twice and quit! *Raycliff* immediately headed for the rocks with what little forward motion she had. Matt and I immediately grabbed the oars and locked them over the side, and against her hull, to try to force her that last ten feet past the rocks, but the oars just slipped past the rocks. I made the quick decision to go over the side and hold her off the rocks so Matt could inch her forward into the harbor. I braced my feet on the rocks and pushed against the starboard side as hard as I could. She moved a little, and then my feet slipped on the moss-covered rocks, and I ended up on my butt in the water. At this exact time, a wave hit her and lifted her up and over my legs. I felt the hull touch my legs, but it did not crush them, as it should have. I wasted no time scrambling to my feet. This time I put my back against her, and she stayed off the rocks long enough to slip into calm water. I just collapsed on the shore. I was physically and mentally drained, having come very close to loosing my legs—and possibly my life. Am I crazy? The only thing I can figure is that both my legs were in between rocks, and the rocks actually protected my legs from getting crushed, or God was covering my butt once again, as He has several times in the past. Heck, He had a hand in the trees also, so He gets all the credit this time. Thank you, *Sir!*

After this little adventure, I was weak-kneed, and I had to go to the bathroom; my bowels were in a state of flux—nerves, probably. We had a Luggable Loo with us, so I grabbed it and headed for a nearby stand of saplings for a little privacy. OK, I'll explain a Luggable Loo…It's quite simple, just a five-gallon plastic bucket with a removable plastic toilet seat that is lined with a bio-disposable plastic liner. It's simplicity for a necessity. So there I was, finally relaxing after a traumatic experience and hard few hours. It was just me, my Loo, and the wind in the trees…and the biggest darn bull snake I have ever seen! Lucky for him (and me), he was just passing through. Thank you again, *Sir!*

A couple of hours later, the wind and waves subsided. We put new spark plugs in the motor so it was alive again, and we headed out of our harbor to cover the last few miles to our intended evening camping spot, to hook up with Vicki. As I remember it, it was a peaceful evening, with many stories to tell around the campfire. We all hoped for a better second day. We did have one small casualty. Big John, who has been a good friend over the years, decided to depart that evening. I've never asked him why, and I don't really need to. It had been a rough two days, and I'm sure he had experienced quite enough of our 1800s-style river expedition. Oddly, the rest of the trip was pretty uneventful; at least insofar as near-disasters were concerned.

As we approached Chamberlain, South Dakota, we elected to stay the evening in a modern marina. (That was an interesting sight. A wooden boat based on a two-hundred-year-old design berthed among modern fiberglass pleasure craft.) As usual, a crowd gathered. So we programmed well into the evening. I think everyone thoroughly enjoyed themselves!

The next morning, we began a short journey to the Oahe Dam for our only portage of the trip. Vicki met us with the Big Green Machine just below the dam. We loaded *Raycliff* on her trailer, drove across the dam, and launched her a mile above the dam. There was plenty of daylight left, so we had a quick lunch, which Vicki prepared on our "commandeered" picnic tabletop. Then we headed off, bound for the Big Bend area, about twenty miles upstream from the dam.

As we approached the Big Bend in the Missouri, we were a bit apprehensive. Our concern was not for the river conditions, but we were dropping in unannounced on the Great Lower Brule Sioux tribal ground. We pulled into the first large bay we could find. It had a good boat ramp and a campground. We had not been there for more than an hour when six large men approached us. And it was obvious they were there to talk to us, as they made their way directly around the beach and to our emerging campsite alongside the *Raycliff*.

I was straining the whole time, trying to determine what the mind-set of the men approaching us was, but these guys were very solemn-faced and very quiet. I got a bit nervous as they strode the last few feet. The obvious leader of the group (and I might add, the biggest), walked right up to me and said, "Nice boat, man! Can we go aboard?" with a big smile on his face. I smiled back and drew a silent sigh of relief, as our guests eagerly climbed aboard to examine *Raycliff*.

Our overnight visit with the Brule just went uphill from there. It actually became a three-day layover! **Our exact stopping spot had not been predetermined when we entered the Big Bend, so we had to call Vicki and direct her to our location.** We did not know at the time that the roads on the reservation were crooked and narrow, so when she finally hooked up with us, she was far less than pleased. With a nice boat ramp nearby, we

decided to pull the *Raycliff* out for a quick inspection below the waterline. A couple of the tribal elders came upon us, and one of them suggested that since the boat was out of the water, it would be nice to show it off at a pow-wow being held in town the next evening.

So the next day, we decided to get ourselves on location early, so we would be ready for that evening's festivities. As we were winding our way through town, trying to locate the building where the pow-wow was to be held, Frank spotted a school. With a smile on his face, he nursed the Big Green Machine and the *Raycliff* into the school parking lot. I knew it was no use arguing with him, and besides, I liked a good kid's program anytime. I jumped down from the cab and headed inside to see if they would be interested, but Frank had different plans to announce our arrival, as he dug out the powder and wick for the *Raycliff*'s bow cannon!

So here's the scene. I'm cautiously working my way down the hall of this school building, surrounded by Native American school kids, and obviously standing out like a dead mouse in a punch bowl, while my crazy truck driver friend, or his alter ego, Cpl. Worfington, was preparing to start another white-man invasion in the parking lot. Get the picture? I had finally found the principal's office, and had been shown in to meet with him. As I walked in, he was looking out the window with his back to me. He turned and asked if that was my boat in the parking lot. I said yes and stammered something like we were prepared to do a program for the school if he thought his students and teachers would be interested. His response was a quick, "I bet they would!" He told me that it might take a few minutes to get their attention, make the announcement, and gather the school. And then he asked me what the guy was doing on the bow of the boat. I moved closer to the window, just in time to see Frank lighting the wick on the cannon. I turned to the principal and told him that getting everyone's attention shouldn't be a problem, as his windows rattled and a plume of black powder smoke drifted across the parking lot. This was the beginning of a three-hour delay in our trip to the pow-wow site. We helped the kids and adults one by one onto the deck of the *Raycliff* from a rickety wooden step ladder, and fired the cannon a couple of more times. We generally had a great time! Around 3:00 p.m., we headed off for the pow-wow. That evening, we once again entertained many of the same children and adults onboard, and many new folks as well. **The**

**principal thought it would be great if we could give the kids a short boat ride in the campground harbor, so we made arrangements to make that happen the next afternoon.** Meanwhile, Vicki had wangled us a visit to the tribal council chambers, where they were holding a planning session. We were

being treated like royalty! My initial apprehension of the Brules' outlook on us being on their land had been turned to dismay for having to leave them. We reluctantly pointed *Raycliff's* bow toward the river current, and we headed upstream the morning of our fourth day with the Brule. Our adventure was going just fine.

When we finally arrived in Pierre, we turned into a narrow, manmade channel and followed it to a small bay in a downtown park, just a few blocks from the motel and our first shower in over a week. The rest of the crew was scheduled to show up in a day or so, and my own Mrs. Keelboat was scheduled to show up that evening. When she arrived, we all piled into her car and headed for a steakhouse just outside of town, to plan our activities during Goose Fest that coming weekend. During dinner, we laid out a schedule for the next few days. As it turned out, everyone would be onsite Thursday evening, but Goose Fest did not officially start until Saturday, so what to do Friday? We all agreed that after almost two weeks on the river, we would stay off the boat and just sightsee or kick back and take it easy for a day.

Later that evening, I was reading the expedition journals covering their time in this area. I would do this for each area where we camped, just in case there might be something related to the expedition that would be neat to see or do; after all, we were reenacting Lewis and Clark's travels. Soon I recognized that the Mouth of the Bad River was very near Pierre. That is where the expedition nearly came to an end in 1805, when they encountered some less-than-friendly Teton Sioux. I glanced at the dates of the journal entries concerning the incident and was surprised to discover that our Friday off was going to be the 198th anniversary of that very day! As I went from motel room to motel room banging on doors with this news, I found the response to be universal. Friday we were going to the Mouth of the Bad! When the rest of the group arrived, we asked them what they had planned for Friday. Their responses ranged from using the motel hot tubs to seeing the sights, but when we told them of our plans and why, they all wanted to come along.

Friday morning was sunny but cool, **and there was a low-lying fog over the park's little bay.** We got that old cranky motor running with a change of plugs, and headed down the man-made channel to the river. This channel was about three-quarters of a mile long, and the fog lingered pretty heavily in it.  As we approached the river, the fog blew off, and we turned the *Raycliff* to starboard and into the river's main channel for our two-mile trip upstream to the Mouth of the Bad River. The Oahe Dam must have had the spillways opened up, as the current was choppy and running hard. We beat our way upstream and arrived at the Bad River in about an hour.

As we turned into the Bad River, we noticed some kids playing onshore on the port side. **Frank just *had* to fire the cannon for them, and they just loved it.** When we pulled closer to shore, about fifty yards in, they all came running down to the boat. We visited with them, but there was no way to get them onboard, as we were bumping bottom and were still three feet from shore. The father of one of the kids  had come down with them and was inquiring as to what we were doing and where we were going and such. He told us about some of the local history, which included local lore that about five miles up the Bad River was where the Teton Sioux had their main camp in 1805. We asked him if he thought we could get there in the *Raycliff*. He said there was no way. He had fished the river a lot, and it was only about two feet deep, and there were several small bridges that our mast would never clear.

Once we explained to him that the mast would come down, and that this old girl would float in twelve inches of water, we invited him along. He had to decline, as he and the children had other plans, but he did ask if we would stop at a dock upstream about one hundred yards on our way back, and let the kids get onboard. **We agreed, dropped the mast, and headed up the Bad.**

The trip up the Bad River was interesting, to say the least. This little river, which is no more than fifty feet wide, ran right through a residential area that had been built up on its banks. I'm confident that the largest boat any of them had seen on that river in their lifetime was maybe a fourteen-foot johnboat. When we cruised by in a forty-two-footer, we could see jaws dropping. It just blew their minds! Several came running out of their doors and down to the water's edge for a brief visit as we crept by at about three knots. We told them that we would return in an hour or so and were planning on stopping at the docks on the south bank just past the pedestrian bridge.

We eventually left the residential build-up behind us and found ourselves in a pretty natural environment, with a farm building spotted here and there. It was all hilly banks or wide-open fields, neither of which would be a good site for an encampment. We were about to turn around and head back, as the river was narrowing, and I had some concerns about actually turning around without grounding, when we spotted a plateau. **We pulled up to the steep bank and climbed up about eight feet, and there before us was a beautiful site for a major encampment.** Protected from the prevailing

winds, grass-covered, flat, and near a good water source. Now we have no proof that this was the site of the main Teton Sioux encampment of 1805, but we're convinced it sure could have been!

Turning the *Raycliff* around required un-shipping the rudder/sweep, and then we were just able to work her 180 degrees with the oars and push-poles, with about two feet of water to spare, between the bow and the bank. An hour later, we passed under the pedestrian bridge and noticed a crowd of about one hundred people on the south side of the river. It looked like we needed to get

into programming mode, so Frank headed for the bow canon with powder and wick. Go figure! **We had a good time with the kids and adults who had gathered,** and about an hour later we nosed her into the Missouri River current and headed downstream to the channel entrance into our safe

harbor for the weekend and for the last few days of our trip. Soon old *Raycliff* would be behind the Big Green Machine headed down the interstate for Onawa. This year's adventure would be over, and who knew what the future would hold. I knew that these river trips were costing Cathy and me thousands, and that it might not be sustainable in the future.

The narrow channel leading to the park area and small bay was running at an angle to the river. It emptied into the river at about a thirty-degree angle pointing downstream, with a small current of its own, due to an inlet from the river at its north end. This mild current was engineered to keep the water fresh in the bay for park-goers. We needed to approach it from the downriver side, so since we were running downstream, we needed to turn almost 180 degrees and 100 feet below the entrance, so we could enter it correctly and safely. This would be pretty simple for modern heavily pow-ered pleasure boats, but old *Raycliff* had marginal power and little steering at slower speeds. Matt was at the tiller, and I was on that cranky motor, as we approached the area and prepared for this tricky maneuver. As we began the port turn, I opened up the throttle. With smoke rolling, we swung around and got pointed upstream toward the channel entrance. Our headway was slow, as the current was very heavy, but we did manage to sneak into the entrance. With a sigh of relief and the sun setting, we started up the three quarters of a mile channel to the safety of the bay. I kept the throttle open until we were safely at least a hundred feet into the channel. As I throttled back, that old motor just quit! It wasn't long before we began to drift back toward the river, and try as I may, I could not get her started. I relayed to the crew that if we slipped out into the river at night, without any power, we would be in dire peril, and instantly three of the guys bailed over the side with ropes and began cordelling us to the safety of the bay. This had been one heck of a day, and we all were beat but satisfied with our adventure as we tied the *Raycliff* up at the dock.

**We spent the weekend giving boat rides and living history programs to folks who attended Goose Fest.** We determined that the old, forty-horsepower motor was now a boat anchor, so we jerked her out and replaced her with a ninety-pound thrust trolling motor. A couple of twelve-volt marine  batteries later, we were underway in the lagoon, albeit slowly, and made it through the weekend.

During this time, we met many interesting folks, including a woman who ran a science museum nearby. She was kind enough to give us a tour of the facility, which was the city's old power station, complete with overhead cranes that amazingly still functioned. Solar-powered cars and home-built aircraft hung from the ceiling. It was a real neat place. I said that all they needed now was a boat like the *Raycliff* displayed right dead center of it all. This gal's eyes lit up when I made this comment. She took us to the back of the facility and showed us an entrance that was about the width of a single car garage. We began discussing what we could do, and when it all washed out, I agreed to loan *Raycliff* to the museum for one year (which ended up being two) as long as we could actually get her in through that entrance.

With tape measures in hand, we set out to see if we could complete this deal we had cooked up. **Two days later, with just inches to spare, we slipped *Raycliff* into her new home for the next two years among all the modern means of transportation. The ceiling was high enough we could put the mast up, sail and all.** As I left the museum on our last day in Pierre, I looked back at my old girl, and I promised that I would be back for her. We were both sad, but she knew I would return.

# Chapter Five

# So Many Projects, So Little Time

During the winter of 2001–2002, we had been heavily into negotiations on some various projects related to Lewis and Clark. The first one to come to fruition was with a movie company shooting a special for a series featured on the History Channel called "Modern Marvels." We were to be featured in a segment entitled, "The Technology of the Lewis and Clark Expedition." We were excited for the opportunity!

Catherine and I had been anticipating being able to perform some hull design testing for quite some time. We wanted to look at handling characteristics of a couple different designs, cargo capacities, and drafts. Our own homemade tank testing facilities were fine for some experiments, but we knew wave generation and underwater photography would require much more sophisticated testing equipment. And now we were being presented with the opportunity to have one of the leading hydroponics testing facilities in the country at our disposal and on someone else's dime! Are you kidding me?

The hydroponics testing lab was located at the University of Michigan in Ann Arbor. The test lab at the university was right at a hundred years old. We were told that the original hull design for the battleship *Arizona* was tested there in the early 1900s. They were currently studying wave action on shore-mounted wave generators, and they had just finished with some high-speed hull designs for the navy. This place was full of fascinating stuff!

When doing this shoot, I wanted to be able to address some important questions about the boats of the expedition, but soon found out that movie-making does not necessarily hinge on one's individual wants and wishes. We did acquire some serious data from our time in Ann Arbor, but most of the technically accurate footage ended up on the cutting-room floor, as did most of the points I had wanted to make about the boats during my "on-camera" interview. When I had discussed these issues with the producer, I was told that they did not want to address any controversies surrounding the subject of the boats. I had been hoping that they would have presented all of the available information on the boats, and let the audience decide for themselves. The material that aired was not what I would have wanted, but the needs of Hollywood won out, as I had no say in how the footage was edited.

Oh, well! Live and learn. On the bright side, we did get the chance of a lifetime at the testing laboratories, and we did make good use of our "off-camera" time.

*Knowledge Nook*
*Testing – Ann Arbor Hydroponics Laboratory*

*A major part of the boat segment was to center around some extensive testing of handling characteristics and hull design. **I very carefully constructed two test hulls, one with a round-bottom profile and the other with a flat-bottom profile. I had one common deck and cabin section that could easily be fitted to either hull.** This would ensure conformity for both test models. At the suggestion of the staff at Ann Arbor, I used a two-inch to one-foot scale; or one-sixth of actual size. The finished models were 110 inches long. The lab technicians determined a scale speed and weight for the models, and we confirmed this with information we had gathered from our full-size replicas. These formulas would be put to good use at our shop facilities that winter in Onawa.*

*We were hoping to collect a lot of test data, which could shed some light on many of the questions surrounding the keelboat. Both the lab technicians and*

*I wanted to do some serious testing, but the film crew just wanted "good footage." **When it was all said and done, we had filmed the boats below the water, at the water line, and from above, all while being rocked, towed, and sunk!** The towing tests conducted for the cameraman were at*

*various speeds. Funny, the lowest of these speeds was probably three times the speed that the actual boat ever moved through the water. At one point, the model looked like a high-speed attack destroyer! So with the film crew happy, we finally got to proceed with some serious testing on the subject of stability.*

Utilizing some rather sophisticated electronics, the lab crew tested both of the hull designs for their ability to handle offset loads, such as shifting deck cargo. Deck cargo is any cargo stowed at or above the waterline. This would include crewmembers at an estimated 150 pounds each. To accomplish this, they installed **an electronic incline meter and a rail attached across the deck amidships.** A pre-calibrated weight was moved from centerline out in predetermined increments, **and the list of the boat noted electronically.**

There are two kinds of stability on a boat: initial stability and reserve stability. Initial stability is what you feel when you step onboard a large boat, or better described as what you don't feel. You don't notice the boat moving under your feet like you would in a

113

small dingy. Reserve stability is what brings ocean sailing boats back upright after they have been blown completely over. In the case of the expedition's keel-boat, the difference between these two types of stability quickly become apparent due to the boat's length-to-width ratio, which is less than many canoes. I am confident that everyone has seen or experienced a canoe's (for lack of a better word) "tipsiness" if you don't stay on the centerline when getting in or out of it.

The tests were centered on deck cargo shift, and how it would affect the list angle of the boat. The question was: Just how much of a list could these designs take before catastrophe would strike? The scenario might go something like this: Say the cordelle line was attached high on the mast to avoid shore debris, and the boat swung out of control, crossways to the current. Your deck cargo has shifted, and all hands are trying to get it back where it belongs. In the process, they have added their combined weight to that side of the boat. The question then becomes how much of a shift in the center of gravity will cause an uncontrollable list, which would result in a capsized craft? Over the years, I had formed some theories about the stability of these craft. I must say that I was quite pleased to see my ideas appear to hold true.

### In a nutshell, this is what we discovered...

The round-bottom design lacked terribly in initial stability, but had a lot of reserve stability. The flat-bottom design had a lot of initial stability and very little or no reserve. All deck cargo and crew would need to stay rather low in the round-bottom design to ensure stability. On the flat-bottom design, this same weight could be safely carried much higher on the boat. A weight shift on the round-bottom design would instantly and dramatically affect the list, but on the flat-bottom design, it had minimal effect. This indicated that the flat-bottom boat was a more stable deck cargo craft than the round-bottom. Even though the round-bottom design was very unstable when subjected to deck cargo, there was a clear indication that if the cargo could be stowed low in the boat, like it is in ocean-going vessels with a deep hold, then the stability of the craft would be excellent. Unfortunately, rivercraft must be shallow draft, which leaves no room for a deep hold. There is a positive side to the round-bottom design. If the boat is "knocked down" by wind or other forces, she will right herself if she doesn't lay there too long and fill with water. By comparison, the flat-bottom design will quickly lose all stability at about forty-five degrees of list, and will easily roll on its side from that point on. Once down, she will just lay there, fill with water, and sink.

### An interesting side note

*The now-famous mountain man, Jim Bridger, experienced this in the 1820s while on his first major expedition to the mountains. Somewhere around present-day Saint Louis, he was aboard the keelboat "Enterprise" when it broke its towrope, hung its mast on an overhanging tree, turned on its side, and sank, no doubt due to a major cargo list inside her hull. She is still there today, and I know of at least one group of people who believe they may have found her. They have contacted me for my estimation as to how they would find her. My response was, "More likely than not, on her side."*

*The other tests we executed had to do with waves and their effect on the hull shapes. Every body of water has its own particular wave pattern. The boys at the lab have most of these loaded on their computer and can simulate just about any kind of ocean or lake wave they want in any kind of wind conditions. I know from experience that rivers also have varying types of waves, depending on the flow rate, volume, depth, wind direction, and wind intensity. Basically it boils down to this: The Missouri River has three different wave scenarios: blowing upstream, blowing downstream, and blowing cross-stream. All of which will react differently to water depth and current flow.*

*A crosswind doesn't affect the wave action to a great degree, although it does make boat handling a bit tough. Winds blowing upstream, or downstream, do create some very dramatic wave patterns, and the more wind, the more dramatic they are. And it seems that the winds always blow on the Great Plains, which as you know, is the home of the "Muddy MO." You get turned sideways to some of these bad boys, and you can be in a world of hurt very quickly! A strong wind blowing upriver can be a good friend and a big help alongside your sail. That same wind blowing downstream can cause a rolling wave action that is a danger to your boat if you were to say, ground the bow on a sandbar and wheel her around to where the wind and its accompanying long-rolling swells hit your craft sideways. In a flat-bottomed, brown-water boat, you would be in great peril.*

*The round-bottom design handles these much better than the flat-bottom. In the rounded hull, the craft slides from one trough to the next with a minimum of roll. The flat design will roll into each successive trough with ever increasing gyrations until catastrophe strikes. If you think about it, this is precisely why rivercraft never venture out to sea.*

*Our rented time at the test laboratory over, we packed up our models and valuable data, and the film crew packed up their footage of our nineteenth-century speedboat. We all left Ann Arbor behind. I was hoping to conduct some additional tests, but we had just run out of time.*

*Determined to continue with testing, we made plans to continue our testing in our tank at home. I wanted to explore some load and draft tests, and work with the cordelle line configurations. The historical information on cordelling is sketchy at best, and we wanted to test some ideas that we had developed on the river in cordelle situations we had experienced.*

## Now, where were we?

From Ann Arbor, we cut cross-country, bound for Charlottesville, Virginia. I was to assist and guide some volunteers who had formed a group to replicate an expedition keelboat/barge. They had put together most of the keel, but their efforts had ground to a halt at that point. I may point out here that most amateurs who try to build a complex boat never finish it. A cliché to be sure, but it does look a lot easier than it is.

We met with the folks the first day, and planned our next two weeks. Fran was in charge. He was a lawyer, a big name in a local law firm. He was a nice guy, and always positive, sometimes too much so for a cautious Iowan. Nevertheless, we meshed well and continued to work well together during our numerous other visits to help them with their project over the next six years.

I spent that week getting them started with building frames in a jig, and left them to continue with that part of the project. I have heard pilots say that flying is hours and hours of boredom separated by moments of stark terror. I would have to say something similar about our numerous visits to Charlottesville over the years. Hours of hard work separated by moments of "Oh, my God, I can't believe we did that!"

The third trip to Charlottesville, we were ready to turn the completed hull over so that the boat could get finished. The hull was built out of one-and-a-half-inch oak and weighed about five tons. And it was left to me, my bride, and a couple of helpers to get her on her keel. We scrounged up some used telephone poles and built two giant sawhorses in the old tobacco barn where we were working. They were about eighteen feet long, so we used block and tackle to raise them after assembly. The old barn creaked quite a bit, but held, and we got them all in place. **We then rigged the four chain hoists along with the chain under the hull and began the lifting process. Taking it ever so slowly, and taking many breaks to let things settle in before lifting a bit further, we eventually had her nearly on her side.**

This is the crucial moment, as you have to transition from lifting to lowering. In order to accomplish this, the hull has to go past the center of gravity point, usually not more than seven or eight inches. Now, this doesn't sound like much of a distance to travel, but when it is five tons of wood hanging from makeshift A-frames, it gets interesting very quickly. Usually we are outside when we pull this tricky maneuver off, but this time we were in a rather confined space. Two of my helpers had never done anything like this before, and had been extremely apprehensive since the beginning of the process. I had told them that when this hull transitioned, it would shake the A-frames and most probably the building itself, as we had the frames attached to the building for added stability. I would have sent them out of the building and done it myself, but I needed some extra hands, so I convinced them there was no danger.

One of the guys, Nate, was especially skittish, but agreed to stick with me. I stationed Nate at the back of the building, as it was the safest spot. You might think that up front by the open door would be best, but the whole rig was leaning that way a bit, and if it were to come down, it would have gone that direction. I climbed onto the upturned hull and secured a large nylon rope to the upper gunnel. Then we had to pull her past center. This was my job. I attached the nylon rope to a come-along and started pulling, all the time keeping a very careful eye on everything. If things went south, I had almost nowhere to go, as it was coming toward me! In case you're wondering, I had Catherine stationed way outside, taking pictures. I told her to get no closer than where I had stationed her, which was ten feet beyond where the whole rig would land if it came her way.

So here's the picture: the rope I was pulling on was strained tight, the hull was just a fraction of an inch from dropping over center, and I estimated that it would probably travel about six inches before being pulled up short by the chains on the down side. At one point I tried to figure out just how many tons of force a five-ton hull would have as it quickly fell from a dead start through the six inches to the chain cradle. I was coming up with figures that scared the hell out of me, so I stopped—stopped figuring, that is. We were turning this hull no matter what!

I shouted out, "OK, here she goes!" as she started that slow-motion trip across that six-inch space. As she hit the restraints, the whole building shook, and many years of accumulated dust and debris came down. It seemed for a second like one of Oklahoma's great dust storms of the 1930s. Mission accomplished! I answered Catherine, as she was hollering in the open door if I was OK, and I was also asking if everyone else was OK.

Everyone answered except Nate. After a few minutes of screaming for him, he came wandering in the front door, having walked around the barn from the rear where he had been stationed. There was no door at the rear of this barn, but upon closer inspection, we realized that there was now! **We all went outside and laughed ourselves sick.**

Since our weeklong visits to Charlottesville were mostly filled with just hard work, which was separated by a few hours of craziness, we shouldn't leave any out. Two incidents of craziness stand out: the turn-over of the hull, which led to a ventilated barn, and the next one, about a year later, when Fran had planned on having the boat launched for the first time during a media event. The terms "media event" and "first boat launch" should never be used in the same sentence. Particularly in this case, as the boat was not yet completed enough to launch, and the chosen launch site was a dubious choice at best.

The Rivanna River is behind and below the work barn, maybe a quarter mile as the crow flies. Down a steep hill and through a soccer field, and then through the trees and shrubs growing along the banks of the Rivanna, makes it more like a half mile. And just in case you were wondering, there was no road through the shrubs and trees, but there is now! Permission from the city to carefully cross the soccer field and to remove a few shrubs was left up to my interpretation. And as the locals would point out, I'm a Yankee from Iowa! Besides, pulling an eight-ton boat and two-ton trailer across a soccer field "carefully" doesn't make them any lighter or the wheel ruts any shallower. As far as the description of a shrub is concerned, where I come from, we have huge cottonwoods, so if it isn't over one foot in diameter, it's a shrub.

When Fran finally saw to what degree I had altered the environment of the area, he was a bit frantic. His response as I remember was, "Well, we'll probably have to fix this when we're done." OK, Fran, is that before or after the "media event" with all the local dignitaries and the press? Oh, well, Cathy and I had a job to do, so we tore into it. Once the area was cleared enough to gain access to the intended launch site, we had to get the boat and trailer down there, plus the A-frames we had built for the turnover. As we would have to spend a few days finishing the boat enough to even consider launching her, time was of the essence. To speed things up, Cathy and I determined that moving the A-frames to the launch site intact would be a huge savings in time. The problem was that they were large and very heavy.

**I designed a bracket system off the hard points on the front of my truck.** We would pull the A-frames over with a nylon rope and hope it didn't break apart. (It didn't.) We put the old girl in four-wheel drive and drug the A-frame to the launch site, which sure raised a lot of dust. Yes, we did drag them across the soccer field, but we were careful. Does that count?

Once we got our non-invasive road graded with a Bobcat, the local groundskeeper, **Terry, helped us set the A-frames up with his tractor.** Oddly, he never said much about what we were doing, or the work we were making for him. **Once we had the A-frames set up, we turned our attention to getting the boat finished and ready for this grand launch.**

After we left the previous autumn, the volunteer group had successfully completed the lockers on the main deck and part of the gunnel. Cathy and I would need to complete the gunnel, cabin, and rudder, and we could only spend about three days getting it done. **Most of the cabin work was from a ladder,** so that slowed us down, and frequent visits from Fran usually added something extra to do. Fran seems to think I am some kind of magician, as there is no limit to what he thinks I can accomplish. I, on the other hand, readily see the limits, and

more of them every day as I get older!

We did accomplish the work on time. **And on the fourth day, we rolled her out for her short trip down to the Rivanna River bank. We carefully backed her down our "road" and positioned her under the two A-frames.** The next step was to get *Discovery Virginia* off the trailer. **Using the same lifting equipment we had turned the hull over with, Cathy and I rigged the lifting straps and hoisted nine tons of boat clear of the trailer. We then quickly removed the trailer, lowered the boat down to about twelve inches off the ground, and left her there for the night.**

**The next day was Saturday, so we would have professional lawyers and doctors helping all day long. Oh, goodie, that should make things go a little slower. We drug in some brand-new telephone poles and put them in position on the hillside running down to the river.** Because of the limited space at the launch site, and the steepness of the bank, we decided that a sideways launch was going to be required.

I was hoping that it would go smoothly and not resemble a nine-ton log rolling down a hill. Once all the skidway logs were in place, we wanted to grease them, but the environmentalists in the group freaked out. So we went to a local grocery store and made probably their largest single sale of cooking grease they've ever had. The next day was the big event, and we had done all we could to get ready for it. If the plan went well, we would be heroes. If not…nope, that was not going to happen!

Fran had lined up a rather large backhoe tractor to assist with the launch. **He came across the soccer field and down our "road" very carefully and positioned himself on the port side of the boat.** In order to get there, he had to remove another couple of "shrubs," but once again he was "careful" as he ripped them out by the roots. Initially *Discovery Virginia* moved right along, albeit only about four feet. Then she hung up at the keel while transitioning from one rail to the other. She was a little unstable at this time, so I

had the backhoe put its bucket against one side, and **we put a chain across the other gunnel to stabilize it.** Someone would have to go under this teetering monster and saw away the offending rail. One of our volunteers, Jim, tried to talk me out of it, but there was no other way to get her moving again. **As I inched myself under the boat, I noticed Jim had followed me down and was kneeling just behind me.** Later, when I asked him what he was doing, he told me that if that boat had moved at all, his plan was to drag me out of the way. At the time, I was a fit 198 pounds and not yet sixty years old. Jim was a rather large boy and spent most of his time behind a desk. Although I do admire his spunk, I was instantly reminded of the last port for *Raycliff* back in 2001, when I ran my "helper" down while scrambling to get a line

on a piling. Lucky for both of us, she did not move.

With that problem averted, **we moved her down the eco-friendly greased logs.** The stern was at about the halfway point on the suspended telephone pole when I heard a sickening snap. **As the stern dropped about two feet, the bow popped up, and she stranded herself on the hillside at about a fifty-degree angle with the stern down near the water.** OK, it was head-scratching time. The dignitaries were all looking at their watches, and we were far from the water. My main concern was that she would roll onto her side and enter the water on her side or even capsize. She probably would not float too well upside down. **We had to do some major re-rigging, and from here on in this was really going to get dicey.** I suggested that we hold a modified ceremony, and get the dignitaries and press out of there. Luckily, cool heads prevailed, and in about an hour we had most of the VIPs and local press out of our hair. And I had formulated a plan of attack.

I rigged some ropes to hopefully prevent her from rolling, and we used pry bars and manpower to inch her toward the water. Finally, she straightened out a bit, and it looked

like success was at hand, when the stern just gave loose and splashed into the river. Now it was all hands on deck, as the water was pouring into the boat through the open cabin windows. We had to get that bow down! We all threw ourselves at it, and down it went. She was afloat at last, about five hours late and half full of water, but afloat!

Soon everyone wanted to take her down the river. I was more than a little concerned about this, as she had a lot of sloshing water in her, but I might as well have been trying to launch a nine-ton boat sideways down a steep bank...wait a minute—been there, done that. **I did insist on life vests for everyone, and away they went in triumph. Wearing my new medal around my neck and a big smile, I put this one behind**

me and had to say to myself, "Oh, my God, I cannot believe we just did that!"

### Knowledge Nook
### Additional Testing – Onawa / Winter 2003

*During the winter of 2003, we completed the second phase of model testing on the Lewis and Clark Expedition barge/keelboat hull. This part of the testing was completed at our shops at the Lewis and Clark State Park near Onawa, Iowa. We drew upon some information we collected during our time in Ann Arbor, and with the help of some other folks, we were able to complete this phase of the testing. I want to thank Mike Butler, Vicki and Frank Koeppe, and my daughter Wendy. Our results follow.*

### Phase One: Cargo capacity / draft tests

*Formula: Weight of the full-size craft, divided by the cube of the scale, equals the scale weight of the model or its cargo. The weight of the scale model or its cargo, multiplied by the cube of the scale, equals the full-size weight. We were working with one-sixth scale models of the barge/keelboat for both hull shapes: round-bottom and flat-bottom. This scale equates to a physical size of two inches to one foot. The completed models were 110 inches long and 16 5/8 inches wide.*

*When we talk about known factors, normally they are known beyond the shadow of a doubt. In the case of this craft, we had to start with a known we could only prove by the preponderance of the evidence. This known factor was the empty weight of the full-size craft. I have built both the flat-bottom and the round-bottom versions of this craft using traditional plank-on-frame methods. Both of these craft weighed in at approximately 10 1/2 tons or 21,000 pounds. Since the original barge/keelboat has been lost to history, we cannot know for absolute certain its weight. However, since I have built several, I feel we are pretty close.*

*Some would argue that by changing the size of the scantlings (framing) and the thickness of the planking, we could drastically affect the finished weight. This is basically a true statement, but it does not take into account some very important boatbuilding basics. Namely, there are limits to how light you can build a boat. But on the opposite side, you can build just about as heavy as you want to. However, if you're building a boat that must have shallow draft and flexibility, but still be strong enough to not fall apart on the first sandbar, you are tied into a certain size range. Also, when a wooden vessel reaches a certain* size, the wood will not be strong enough to hold it together. It's kind of like the string-in-the-hole question.

How far could you lower an endless roll of string into a bottomless hole? The answer is that you could only lower it as far as its tensile strength would allow. When the string in the hole outweighs the tensile strength of the string itself, it will break, and your experiment will be over.

Wood also has a tensile strength, and this rule applies after the mass of the object exceeds a certain point. Remember, a wooden vessel, unlike a house, has no foundation to sit on other than the fluid environment it sits in. This environment, if absolutely calm, supports the structure rather well. However, it is often far from calm. The stresses a boat hull endures are much more diverse than the stress a house is subjected to. This problem was partially solved in the mid to late nineteenth century by adding iron straps and such, and eventually an iron frame, covered, by wood. Although these practices were widely commonplace by 1850, they were not in the boatyards along the rivers fifty years earlier. Salt-water deep draft ships utilized some of these metal fittings, but rivercraft construction didn't see much of it until just before the Civil War.

If you have a moment, compare the size of a certain historically important vessel measured in "cubits" to the size of the largest wooden vessel ever built without metal substructure, and you will understand the meaning of the term "unquestioning faith."

You might ask yourself, "How does this apply to your replicas being of an accurate weight?" What all this does is limit the size range of scantlings and planking that would apply historically to a replica, and also would affect the spacing of the scantlings as far as the craft being flexible, rather than rigid. Here is what it boils down to in layman's terms:

The scantlings (frames) of the craft would be spaced anywhere from 2 to 2 1/2 feet apart. They would probably be anywhere from 3 to 4 inches square. Part of this sizing on the frames is allowance for a number of fittings, metal or wood per frame per plank. The planking would have to be heavy enough to not be punctured by obstacles encountered, yet light enough to maintain the shallow draft and flexibility requirements, without being dangerously under-built. In my opinion, we would have to be at least 1 1/2 and up to 2 1/4 inches thick.

When we do all of the fancy math, mixed with my opinions, we come up with a boat that weighs as little as 9 1/2 tons and as much as 11 tons. The ones we built have been tested in the water under many conditions and are mid-range in this design field. They have approximately 3x3-inch frames, spaced 3 feet apart, with 2-inch planking on the bottom and 1 1/2 inches on the sides. The wood used is oak. You could use a softer, lighter wood, but then *you would have to use more of it and space the frames closer, so it is about a wash on wood used. OK, that's why I feel comfortable using 21,000 pounds as a base figure. The finished model weighed 96 pounds. This was 1 1/5th pounds shy of the 97 1/5 pounds predicted by our formula based on the 20,000 pounds figure. This was determined to be a result of the model's construction materials, basswood and fiberglass. The combination of these two items results in a strong and easily built model, but not necessarily an accurate scale weight. At this time, I better understood the comments made by the Ann Arbor lab folks. I was, quite frankly, very pleased with myself. We ballasted the models to the predetermined scale weight and began our experiments.*

*NOTE: **Each model was in two parts, the hull and a common superstructure, which would fit tightly on each.** The weight of this superstructure was predetermined in advance, and then **figured into the weight of the complete model. We felt that the ballast tests would be easier if we had unfettered access to the open hull, so we ballasted for the superstructure and removed it for the testing.** The*

*weights we used were plastic bags of sand that had been filled and weighed prior to the testing. They were in 20, 10, 5, and 1 pound units.*

### Here are the results of our tests:

*The round-bottom version of the keelboat would draft 4 to 4 1/2 feet of water with 12 tons of cargo. With the same amount of cargo, the flat-bottom version would draft 2 to 2 1/2 feet. It was then pretty simple to calculate the additional draft per a given weight of cargo. The ratio would be different between round-bottom and flat-bottom, but each would have its own distinct ratio after a certain draft has been reached due to the hull cross-section shape. Once* you're past the roundness of the round-bottom design and the square chine of the flat-bottom design, the 5-degree flair of the sides has little effect on these calculations. We concluded that the round-bottom boat would draft an additional inch for each 1,333 pounds of cargo added. The flat-bottom boat would draft an additional inch for each one 1,500 pounds of cargo.

### Phase Two: Cordelle Tests

Our test tank in Onawa was 40 feet long and 3 feet wide. We conducted extensive cordelling tests at various speeds and with many different types of rigging. Our rudder was equipped with a protractor so angles of the rudder could be noted at various speeds and with different cordelling rigs. One of the problems facing us with our limited equipment was how to figure scale speed. First you have to understand that scale speed through the water in a test tank is not necessarily the actual or "true" speed the original or a full-size replica might be making on the river. It would first depend on if you were going with the current or against it, or if you were in "slack" water. If you are moving against a 4-mile-per-hour current making a hull speed of 6 miles per hour, then you're actual or true speed is 2 miles per hour. To test the way the boat hull reacts to cordelling rigs, rudder angles, and various tow speeds, you must scale your tank tests to a 6-mile-per-hour figure, which is the speed of the water past the hull. Water moving past the wetted surface of the hull is important to these tests. I was rudely introduced to something called "The Reynolds Number" and coefficients of drag for fresh water. I'll not bore you with them here, though. Heck, I still don't really understand them, but I found someone who did... my oldest daughter, Wendy. In her job as a chemical engineer, she routinely works with this stuff, and pitched in to help me out. The long and short of it is that we towed the models at a "scale hull speed" of 8 miles per hour. I picked this speed because I felt it best represented the average true hull speed of the full-size boat against the Missouri River conditions encountered by Lewis and Clark. My crew has cordelled the full size replica on moving and still water, and their speed has been noted using a GPS unit. The journals record times and distances traveled, but not much about current speed.

The speed of the current is very relative. It would depend on whether you're in the main channel, the inside of a bend, or the outside of it. Also the width of the river would affect the speed. Current is also impacted if it's a mile wide meandering through various small islands or choked down to 40 feet due to debris. I believe that the average current Lewis and Clark dealt with was between 3 and 5 miles per hour. The other factor that comes into play is that our tests showed that hull speed was not as much a factor in controlling the boat, as was the actual cordelling ropes, and how they were rigged. For these reasons, I feel that our scale tow speed has yielded pretty honest results.

At any given time during the cordelling operation, the shoreline might be clean and smooth, choked with debris, have a steep bank, or who knows what else. The object for the personnel doing the cordelling was to keep the rope taut, and maintain the best footing they could, whether it was in or out of the water. Through our full-size reproduction, reenactments, and these tank tests, I have developed some theories on the subject of cordelling a large boat on the Missouri River.

The basic concept is similar to the string attached to a standard kite. One string off the top and one from the bottom meet at a point approximately two-thirds the distance from the bottom of the kite and about one-thirds the distance from the face. At this location, the line is attached to the operator on the ground. By shortening or lengthening either of the two strings attached to the kite, you alter the angle at which the kite flies. More tilt forward for light breezes and less for stronger ones. If you turn the kite on its side, and replace it with a boat, you can see the similarity.

The preponderance of the evidence I have uncovered shows that in a complicated cordelle with ever-changing river and shoreline conditions, at least a five-man cordelle crew onboard would be required for the safe passage and control of the boat. In other cases, where the water and shoreline are much more benign, one man could safely handle the cordelle aboard. In the simplest of scenarios, you would have a single line from the mast or gunnel to shore, fixed in its position. The water conditions and shoreline are constant and non-threatening. In a complicated cordelle situation, it might go like this: **The main cordelle line is attached to the mast, which is about two-thirds of the way from the rear of the boat.** It is then passed through a ring, which is in turn tied to a rope, which passes through another ring on the bow of the boat. We will call this the "ring line." The cordelle line would more likely than not be attached to the yard, so that it could be easily raised and lowered as needed to clear obstacles on the river. A man would probably be stationed at the base of the mast, to instantly change the

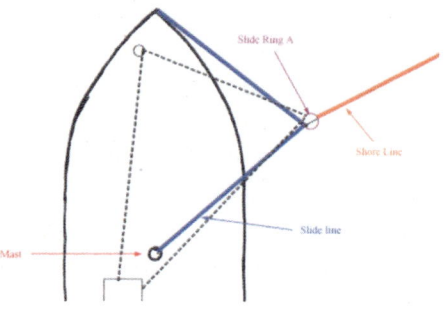

*height of the main cordelle line when needed. Another man would probably be stationed at the bow on the ring line. His job would be to bring it in or let it out to change the angle of attack of the bow of the boat, to accommodate different hull speed changes, due to faster or slower current or faster or slower cordellers. A third man stationed probably between these two would help where needed. With the pressure of the cordelle rope on the mast yard, it would be a bear to raise or lower (using a pull down line), and the same would be true of the line through the bow ring. If I were handling that line, I would take a turn or two on the mooring bit so I could pay it out with some control as needed, and would call for help if I had to haul it in a bit. I would probably have my hands full trying to throw a loose roll off the mooring bitt, while at the same time not losing too much slack in the line. If someone were to momentarily pinch off the line at the bow ring, I could quickly slip it off the mooring bit and lock it down until my helper could latch onto it with me to haul it in.*

*While these three guys are busy, a fourth man with a setting pole might be very useful to help hold the bow against the current until the rope handlers could get squared away. Each of these crewmembers is under the control of the tiller man. He and he alone can see if the bow of the boat is swinging to port or starboard. This is a fact: you cannot tell if the bow of the boat is turning left or right from anywhere onboard until it is too late to stop it, unless you're at the stern looking down the length of the boat. These five guys, along with whoever could help, would control the boat during a cordelle. They would work in unison under the commands of someone near the stern, most probably the tiller man, and by changing rope lengths and heights, would keep the boat out of harm, way and heading upstream under control.*

*The tiller man could under most conditions keep the boat under control with just the rudder. If he saw that he was losing her to port or starboard and couldn't correct the swing with the rudder, he would call down to the ring man to let more line out or take some in. Once the boat was on more of a "balanced centerline," he would once again regain rudder control. If he noticed a large debris pile on the bank ahead, he would call for the boom/cordelle line man to raise the boom to clear the obstacles, and then when past them, he would call for the boom to be lowered to a better cordelle angle. The higher the cordelle line on the mast, the less control the rudder has, and the more likely that the tiller would become ineffective, bringing into play the ring line crewmember. The optimum cordelle height is no more than is needed to keep the line out of the water. Once that cordelle line is in the water, the current drags on it, it loses its tensile strength, it stretches, and debris will catch on it. It is much more desirable to keep it above the water and dry, although this is often impossible.*

*Cordelle line length is a real catch 22. The longer it is, the more control you have of the boat left and right with the rudder alone; however, the added length makes it more susceptible to being drug in the water and snagging on debris. By shortening the line, you eliminate these fouling problems, but you lose much of the control over the boat's distance from the shoreline. It is definitely a balancing act. Just in case you think that cordelling was invented for our rivers, think again.* **Among many others, the Chinese have cordelled on the Yangtze River rapids for thousand of years; they call it lining.**

*I present these theories based on experience, testing, and historical research. I strongly urge you to question everything I have said and see if it stands up under your scrutiny.*

## Now, where were we?

While we were wrapping up our testing, I received a call from the head of the parks division for Bismarck, North Dakota. As a result of that conversation, we were setting our course for the next year but would eliminate any chance of getting on the river again in 2003. They wanted a full-size keelboat/barge and the front half of the river steamboat, *Yellowstone*. The *Yellowstone* replica would be the size of a three-story house. They were to be built in Onawa, then disassembled, shipped to Bismarck by July 2003, and reassembled at the edge of the river on pilings. It took most of that winter and into early summer to build these items. They were then shipped to Bismarck in July, and by the end of August, I had all of them installed on site. Nothing particularly spectacular happened during this building and installation time, which was directly related to the work itself, although there was one thing that had some influence on me later concerning the keelboat.

The folks in Bismarck wanted the keelboat twelve feet wide so it would be wheelchair accessible. I had no problem with that, and once built I realized that it didn't really detract from the authentic look of the boat. I also realized that this additional width would make her very stable, and tucked that tidbit of information away for future use. Another interesting thing happened one day near the end of the project. I was on the third deck of the steamboat when my cell phone rang. The gentleman introduced himself and asked if I was the individual who had built the model keelboat in the Heinz Museum in Pittsburgh. Yes, I was, and I asked him what I could do for him. He said that he needed a full-size working keelboat in Pittsburgh in three days. So I asked him what he really wanted, and who had put him up to this. He then reiterated his request and assured me he was deadly serious. I told him that there was the first one I had built in Onawa, Iowa, and it did have a new trailer under it. I warned him that it would cost a lot of money, and I still did not think it would be possible to pull it off, as you could not begin to get all the permits within that time period. He said that money was not a problem and asked whom he should reach out to. I put him in contact with

my good friend, Russell Field, the Department of Natural Resources technician for the park. The next thing I heard was that the boat was on its way to Pittsburgh with some of my old crew, and all obstacles, including permits, were taken care of. I hated to miss that trip, but I had a job to finish.

**When it was all said and done, the keelboat replica, *Discovery*, from our state park, was floating on the Ohio River in downtown Pittsburgh and participating in the kick-off for the Lewis and Clark Expedition Bicentennial.** A gentleman who owned a local football team funded it all. As I heard it, the permit problem was solved with season passes to the games, but you know how rumors are.

The last account from Bismarck involves me getting an award for my work there. I was the only contractor out of three to complete my projects on time and on budget. Now I can tell you, I have always liked being appreciated and will do just about anything for those who show me that kind of respect. Conversely, the opposite of that holds equally true, as some have found out.

## Chapter Six

# Best Friend and the Rest of Our Story

In the winter of 2003–2004, I asked my bride and best friend if I could blow most of our savings and build our own expedition keelboat/barge replica. One just for the two of us and for whatever endeavors present themselves. Basically, anything that I want to try, she most generally supports one hundred percent. Her reasons are her own, but I can tell you that all of my successes in the last forty years are because of her. Without that kind of support, I would be like so many other dreamers: just dreaming and planning but never doing. We have made one heck of a team through mutual support and respect for each other's life ambitions. If anyone reading this thinks they can follow in our footsteps, first find yourself a "best friend," then marry her, twice if need be (we wed again on our twenty-fifth wedding anniversary), and then never look back!

I decided that *Best Friend* would be fifty-eight feet long and twelve feet wide. The extra width was for extra stability. The extra length was for better accommodations in the cabin. These changes wouldn't alter her looks too awful much from the original expedition keelboat/barge, and they made her very safe. The construction technique would be just like the *Raycliff*, and some others I had built since the year 2000, only heavier. The bottom of the hull would be three layers of 3/4-inch treated plywood up to the waterline. Then it would be two layers overlaid with 5/4-inch cedar planking, to the gunnel. The frames (or scantlings) were 4x4-inch treated, spaced about 2 feet apart. When completed, she would weigh right at 12 tons. When it was all said and done, she cost about $30,000 to build.

The construction period was fairly uneventful, except on a couple occasions. Basic construction was just me and a young Nathan Butler, the son of one of our groups members, Mike Butler. Nathan was about nineteen then and would protest daily about working so many hours each day. He worked Monday through Friday, from about 9:00 a.m. to 4:00 p.m. Shop arrival time for me was 6:00 a.m., and I left about 10:00 p.m. This was my routine at least six days a week, if not seven. I've never been known to sit idle for too long.

One of our "eventful" occasions was near the day we were going to turn the hull over. I had called in Nathan's dad, Mike, and **my son-in-law, Kurt Keefe, and some grandkids came along to keep us entertained.** It wasn't as traumatic as the Charlottesville turn over, but it was interesting, to say the least. We were working in a huge Quonset, which yielded little room in which to work, and once again I had employed old telephone poles as homemade A-frames. It was a pretty tight squeeze when she was right at that tip-over point, and just as dramatic when she traveled that short distance into the lowering cradle. The A-frames shook, the building shook, and the grandkids squealed!

Another interesting part of the building phase of *Best Friend* was a phone call I received from some friends in Hartford, Illinois. The summer prior, among all my other projects, **I built one half of an expedition keelboat/barge for them, a "cut-away."** I had shipped it down, and had installed it inside their museum, which was still under construction at the time. The Illinois State Historical Museum is just across the river from Saint Louis, Missouri.

Let's jump off track for a moment, and then we'll get back to the phone call. The design firm who had hired me to build this replica cut-away had initially come to Onawa to visit with me about this project. I showed them our craft and explained my design concepts. (I also wined and dined them, as this project would pay very well.) One of the subjects we discussed at length was the round-bottom design versus the flat-bottom. They whole-heartedly agreed with me.

Imagine my surprise when they came back to finalize the deal with only one catch, they wanted me to follow the round-bottom design. I recovered my composure enough to ask them why the round-bottom. They gave me a response that I have never forgotten. They needed to be able to justify to the State of Illinois where they had gotten their design material. So even though they did agree with me completely, they could not use my design because (Are you ready for this?) I had not published about it, and someone else had. Another darn good reason for this book!

OK, back to the phone call. The folks running the museum were planning a major event for the expedition's bicentennial celebration, and they wanted me to bring my new boat down for it. (The Lewis and Clark community is pretty close-knit, so they had heard of my new project and wanted in on the action.) They asked me how she was coming along, and I told them just fine. I did not mention that I was only two days into it. Neither did I mention that at that very moment, I was standing next to a pile of pre-cut gussets, which was all I had accomplished to date.

We visited about their ideas, and it all sounded like a great way to show off my work to thousands. Also I would have my flat-bottom design just outside the window in Hartford, where the round-bottom model was located. So I asked them what the date of their event was. Their celebration was to be held in just ninety-three days! I was  in the process of explaining to them that there was no way Nathan and I could get her done in time when they mentioned that they had received a substantial grant to get my boat and me on-site for the event. Long story short, on the ninetieth day we loaded her! Money can be quite an incentive.

Frank hooked up to the trailer with his Big Green Machine and headed for Hartford.

To stray even further from our original story, on this particular trip, Frank had estimated a two-day haul to Hartford and ended up running ahead of schedule, so he and Vicki made a small detour. Evidently, they had a nephew who lived in a small town in Iowa close to Interstate 80. So picture this... with no advance notice, Uncle Frank and Aunt Vicki wheel up into this kid's school parking lot with a twelve-ton keelboat. "Cpl. Worfington" proceeds to load the cannon on the bow as Vicki runs inside to warn the principal! A stepladder was procured, Frank went into full Cpl. Worfington mode, and they proceeded to negate the afternoon's school lessons with a very special history lesson of their own. Their program was the hit of the day, and their nephew was a star! I guess Dale and I had been rather successful in our undertaking to transform this kind, middle-aged trucker into a historical programmer. Catherine and I headed to Hartford a day behind them. We secured enough funds to invite some of our old crew along. We would program with reenactors and enlighten people about Lewis

and Clark's journey aboard our replica craft. And, boy, everyone ended up having a great time!

After the big event, *Best Friend* came back to Onawa. A month later, we wetted her for the first time on Blue Lake. Now I had built *Best Friend* for the river to perform some "experimental archeology" and to educate. If that was going to happen, we had to get her on the river! Around this same time, I bumped into a gentleman named Wayne from North Dakota.

Wayne happened to own some property right along the Missouri River, about twenty-seven miles upriver from Bismarck, and seventeen miles downstream from Mandan. Somehow we cooked up this plan to haul *Best Friend* to Bismarck and launch her there within feet of her shore-bound predecessor at the city park. We would then lash a ninety-horsepower boat to her side and power her upstream to his property.

I hooked up with Frank again for the trip up. I also took along a local young man whom I'd been mentoring. "Danny" just needed a friend to lend him a hand and give him a break, and I always enjoy a sidekick. I told him I'd show him a great adventure! We all joined up and headed out.

We arrived in Bismarck too late to launch, so we slept aboard *Best Friend* on the trailer that night. Early the next morning, **we proceeded to get her on the river.** Our first stop was downstream about three miles. We would be heading to a dock where city dignitaries, local news folks, and the general public could come aboard and look her over. When the full-day media event was over, we prepared to head upstream to our new home for the next two months.

Wayne had told me of a Lewis and Clark campsite located on his property, albeit probably near the middle of the river today. The journal entries for this camp mentioned that Captain Clark had a sore neck, which Captain Lewis doctored with a poultice and diagnosed it as rheumatism. So our new

temporary home along the upper Missouri River was subsequently named "Camp Rheumatism."

Danny and I spent the first night on the river aboard *Best Friend*, tied to an island midstream. Meanwhile, our powerboat guide headed back to Bismarck for fuel, with a promise to return for us the next morning. It later dawned on me that if he hadn't kept that promise, we would have been in quite a pickle, because even my cell phone had no signal. Well, of course he did indeed return. We hooked on and set out for Camp Rheumatism, hoping to arrive before dark.

Around noon on that second day, a strange thing happened. A bright orange, Coast-Guard-looking helicopter flew fairly low over us, circled twice, and then flew off. We just could not figure that out at all. How bizarre! Anyway, later that day, we pulled into camp just as the sun was setting that evening. We tied her to two dead men on the shore, had some supper, and went to sleep, very exhausted.

### Knowledge Nook

*When you need to tie your boat off to a shoreline that offers no trees or large rocks, you can dig a hole in the sand and bury a log or the ship's anchor. You then tie off to that. This is called a dead man.*

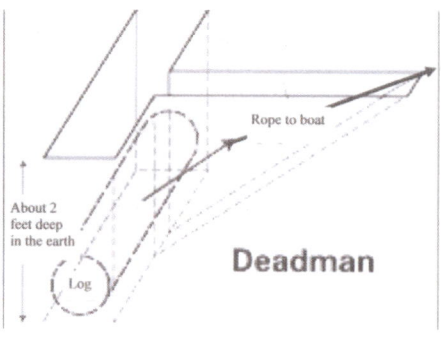

*Later that evening, just after supper, Danny said he had to use the toilet, which I hadn't gotten set up for us yet. But I did have the old tried-and-true Luggable Loo! So I explained the simple process for using old Loo and sent him off. He returned a while later with a bag over his shoulder, complaining that he hadn't taken along a shovel to dig a hole. It was getting late and we were bushed, so I told him to scoop some wet river sand into the bag to weigh it down and just toss it into the river. After all, it was biodegradable, so the river would just dissolve it away for us. So he tossed the bag off the bow. As the bag floated down the side of the boat, I commented that he needed to use a little more sand next time.*

*The next morning, shortly after breakfast, he once again needed old Loo and once again forgot a shovel. So down he came to the boat again with his bag. When he came onboard, I noticed that this time the bag appeared to be half*

*full, and I was hoping that it was mostly sand. Like an Olympic-style shot-putter winding up for his distance attempt, he stood at the bow and proceeded to whirl his bag into the river. On about the third rotation, the ten pounds of "stuff" inside the delicate, lightweight bio-baggie burst asunder in a great cloud of debris. Lucky for me, and the boat, this happened right as it arced toward the river. So (Thank you, Sir, again), it all landed in the water. I stepped back into the cabin, laughing hysterically. I also resolved that getting a port-a-potty on site that day would be my first priority.*

*Our first job was building a counterweighted ramp to the boat so we could easily move it up and down by one person, even though it weighed several hundred pounds. We set up our educational camp, consisting of a Spanish windlass, a blacksmith shop, a woodworking area, and the al-ways-infamous rope-making machine.*

### Knowledge Nook

*The expedition was well equipped. It had a forge, which was necessary to repair items that were broken. The crew also made many metal objects as trade items with the natives. Basic carpentry tools were employed to make new oars, push-poles, and masts when needed along the trail. Also during the expedition, the men did indeed make rope for their own use. They described using elk hides to accomplish this. Rope making differs from braiding and has for thousands of years. Braiding is probably familiar to most. You see it in a girl's pigtails and in bullwhips. Yet rope making is entirely different, as it has always involved twisting its strands in opposite directions to create a tight, strong rope. Most common ropes come in three-strand and four-strand, with three-strand being the most prevalent through the ages.*

*You can take three strands of anything; let's say 1/8-inch-wide strips of elk hide. Twist each of them separately until they are twisted tight, and then reverse your twist pattern and twist them together into one strand. Do this three times. Then take those three strands and twist them together in the opposite direction. You now have a rope. If your rope is large enough, great! If not, make two more of the size you made and twist them together, reversing the direction of the twist to make a larger rope. (I estimate the elk rope used by the expedition members was 2 1/2 to 3 inches in diameter.)*

*Now, while at Fort Mandan during the winter of 1804–1805, Lewis and Clark Expedition members utilized what they called a "Spanish windlass" to help free their boats from the ice of the Missouri River.* **A windlass is generally understood as a cylinder upon which a rope or cable is wound, thus multiplying the force applied to the rope or cable manifold.** *A Spanish windlass is generally understood as a piece of wood or metal inserted between two ropes, which is turned to twist the ropes tight and exert pulling power along the rope's length by effectively shortening the rope.*

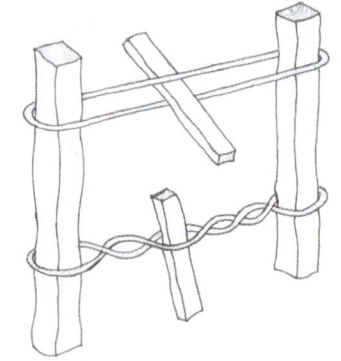

*I believe, based on my years of working with primitive machinery, that it is more likely than not that the expedition members used the basic windlass design,* which utilizes a cylinder to wind the rope on, commonly called a capstan on a ship. If you needed to pull a boat out of the water from the shore, it would definitely do the job. Furthermore, I believe that more than one would have been employed to accomplish this. I have built a couple of these primitive windlasses using hand tools that would have been available to the expedition members. I have estimated that each one would exert a force of one thousand pounds *of pressure on its homemade rope, with ease. Three to five of these could very effectively move a heavy object.*

*My beliefs concerning Lewis and Clark's Spanish windlass beg me to touch on the subject concerning terms used, yesterday and today and during the Lewis and Clark Expedition. Over the years I have had lengthy discussions and arguments over just what the journalists meant about something when they attached a name to it. Was it just a windlass or was it a true Spanish windlass? A true gauge plug, or a drain plug? A spritsail, or jib sail?...And so on. In my opinion, you might as well try to nail Jell-O to a tree as to nail down their meanings!*

### Another example of misunderstood terms

*Have you ever seen the chinking between the logs on a log cabin? Most people will answer, "Yes." But to someone who knows log cabin construction well, they know that they've not seen chinking at all. Chinking is the small pieces of wood used to help close the opening between the logs prior to the application of the mud, concrete, or whatever daubing material is available. What they are seeing is actually the daubing, not the chinking.*

*The list goes on and on. Hearing a term used and being able to apply it in a correct manner is very easy for the professional, but it can be difficult for the amateur. I can see it two hundred years from now: What did he mean when he said PC? Personal Computer or Politically Correct? What about thongs? Footwear or underwear? And I'm confident that if you think about it, you can come up with many of your own. If two hundred years in the future they still have Jell-O and nails, maybe they can also give that a try!*

## Now, where were we?

We had been working to get Camp Rheumatism ready for visitors. This all took a couple of days, so while we were busy getting it built, Wayne was beating the bushes with local schools and setting us up with a temporary post office box. I did not know at the time that he was also lining me up to help teach a college course on pre-steam river travel at Bismarck State University as a guest lecturer. As it turned out, we formed an agreement with the dean of the college. About twenty of their students who had elected to take this Lewis and Clark Expedition course would crew *Best Friend* upriver to Mandan, learning pre-steam river history as a portion of their credit, and

I would be compensated for the use of my boat, lecturing, and captaining the trip upstream. At times, life can be very good!

Oh, heck! My life is always pretty good, and at times outlandishly so! Let me tell you about one of the first pieces of mail we received from our temporary post office box in Bismarck. Having been interviewed by local TV stations and papers that summer, only a recluse would not have known who we were, what we were up to, and where we were. So I wasn't surprised when Wayne dropped off the mail one day, and there was a large manila envelope. It was addressed to the keelboat captain at Camp Rheumatism. Well, remember that bright orange helicopter that circled us on our trip up from Bismarck? There in the envelope was a photo of us, obviously taken by someone in that helicopter.

With it, a short note read: "We received a report of a large dock or barge that had broken free and was floating down the river and a danger to other boaters. We investigated and found you. You seemed to be under control, *sort of*, so we came home. We thought you would like this photo." It was not signed, and I have no idea if it was actually the Coast Guard or just some guy in a bright orange helicopter! Now is that unreal or what?

Around this same time, I met some local guys who seemed to be footloose and fancy-free. They all worked at the local power plant, performing maintenance over the long winter months in North Dakota. During the summer they lived on the river, and they knew every inch of it! It didn't take me long to strike a deal with them and enlist them as extras in an upcoming movie shoot. Mike Lang and Bruce Narveson were the two who stood out in this elite group of river experts. Mike and Bruce were good friends, and I believe that they had been since their youth. They were great sidekicks to have around. Mike was the bold one, and Bruce was the cautious one. It was a pleasure to have them involved, and an honor to know them. It was a great experience sharing this adventure with them. In fact, their contribution to my endeavors on the upper Missouri was invaluable.

I called back to Onawa and got hold of a couple of my old crew and offered to cover their expenses if they wanted to come up for the Mandan trip. My new friends and my old friends did not mesh all too well, but we made it work. Different groups from different worlds, it happens. My bride would also be able to join me for a few weeks and help with a movie shoot, which Wayne had obtained for us. This was going to be a busy, grand time, for sure!

The movie people were a hoot; they always are. I have shot footage with my boats for over thirteen different movie companies, including some of PBS's film crews. Ken Burns's epic Lewis and Clark Expedition documentary, which aired on public TV stations across the nation, utilized all of my boats. If you sit in on the movie "Westward Expansion" shown at the Saint Louis Arch, you will see *Best Friend* in it, and the list goes on. Each movie has a story to tell, and this one was no different.

The movie people arrived with all their own costumes and started dressing all of my volunteer extras. They were shooting a movie about the "Trail of Tears," which befell the Great Cherokee Nation back in the 1800s. At

one point, the white soldiers loaded most of the Cherokee on a keelboat so they could be shipped like cattle to their new (and not of their choice) home; we were to reenact that event. The incident that stands out with this shoot grew out of an attitude that the director wanted from the extras. He wanted hatred and cruelty depicted between the costumed keelboat men and the Native American actors, men, women, and children, all of whom were locals. As the Cherokee were being herded onto the keelboat back in the 1800s, the white men onboard treated them horribly, and if they'd had electric cattle prods back then, they would have used

them. The director wanted to show this uncivilized level of abuse and disrespect. The problem was that these folks all knew each other well and were friends, in some cases relatives.

The first take was a joke, as everyone was cordial and talkative. The director wanted a completely different attitude portrayed, and kept making the actors repeat the scene in the hot afternoon sun. The director berated the extras every time they did a retake, and each time the tensions got a little higher, as all the actors involved became weary of the dozen or more retakes with no break. Finally the actors rebelled and wanted a rest, but the director actually got very short with them and all but ordered them to go one more time. On this last take, one of the white keelboat crew and one of the Native American extras almost got into it when the white guy nearly shoved the Native American onto the main deck. That was it. The director had what he wanted,

but the two men actually went their separate ways for a while. You see, they were best friends and hunting buddies, and would be again, but some wounds take a long time to heal, maybe even a hundred and fifty years or more…

Anyway, the movie shoot over, and it was time for our college student trip to Mandan. We would be the first expedition-style boat to reach Mandan in two hundred years if we could make it! The trip was full of fun and excitement. The real kicker came at the end of it. Some truths just show up and surprise you, and this was my time to get one laid on me. At this time in my life, I had spent nineteen years chasing the ghosts of the Lewis and Clark Expedition without blinking an eye or really thinking about it much. As we pulled up to the docks at Mandan, a local reporter who was curious about how long

it had been since we left Camp Rheumatism hollered down to me, "Hey, Butch, how long did it take you to get here?" My reply, which surprised everyone, including me, was, "Almost twenty years." Sometimes the truth just jumps up and bites you when you least expect it.

### Knowledge Nook

*A Question to Ponder...before we head back downstream from Mandan. (In this section I quote directly from the journals and the letters of the expedition.) On August 30, 1803, Lewis left Pittsburgh with his new barge. The day he left Pittsburgh with his new boat, he wrote this in his journal:*

    *"Left Pittsburgh this day at eleven o'clock with a party of eleven hands."*

    ***While keeping this journal entry in mind, please consider that Lewis's new craft and cargo would have weighed between eight and ten tons. Now let's consider his cargo, which he had been gathering at Pittsburgh for several months. Most have agreed that his cargo weighed between nine and twelve tons, possibly more. Just for the sake of argument, why don't we give***

*him the benefit of the doubt and say he had a mere eight tons of cargo on-board. This would put the combined weight of the boat and cargo between sixteen and eighteen tons.*

*As he traveled down the Ohio River, he discovered that the water was very low due to the lateness of the year and stemming from his boatbuilder's constant delays. He then made the following entry in his journal on the same day as the entry above.*

*"Proceeded to a ripple of McKee's rock where we were obliged to get out all hands and lift the boat over about thirty yards."*

*OK, now, even if Lewis himself helped, that would give every man more than a ton to lift. That's two thousand pounds each, which is equal to the weight of fifty or so cement blocks.*

*Now while your pondering that, let's consider some other comments he made in a letter to Jefferson dated September 13, 1803.*

*"I was obliged to cut a passage through four or five bars, and by that means past them; this last operation is much more readily performed than you would imagine; the gravel of which many of these bars are formed, being small and lying in a loose state, is readily removed with a spade, or even with a wooden shovel, and when set in motion the current drives it a considerable distance before it subsides or again settles at the bottom.".*

*In this entry Lewis is saying that his men could dig a trench in the sand and gravel of a muddy river wide enough and deep enough for an eight-foot-wide boat to slide through. (Keep in mind that they were more than likely working in murky water, which is anywhere from one to two-and-a-half feet deep. Between these two statements, which one do you believe is more likely true: twelve men lifting over twelve tons or more, or digging an eight-foot-wide channel in muddy water with hand tools?*

## Now, where were we?

We were on our way downstream, having just shoved off from Mandan with our crew of college kids. I was about to learn a valuable lesson from my volunteer North Dakota crew and would end up owing one of them more than I could ever repay. We did not overnight at Mandan, so it was already midafternoon before we pointed *Best Friend* downstream toward Camp Rheumatism. We were pretty confident that we could not make it in one day, and we had tentage and food onboard for an overnight along the shore somewhere. We were getting along well under sail and oar, when all of a sudden someone put on the brakes. No warning, no noise, we just stopped! I had felt the tiller lift a bit, but that occasionally happened when we ran over a floating piece of debris, such as a tree limb or who knows what. Heck! It was a partially submerged junk car once!

What would normally happen when the tiller lifted a bit is that the item (whatever it was) would just slide along the keel, and when it got to the rudder it would lift the rudder a bit, due to the slack in the rudder shaft, and then it would just roll under and out behind the boat. You would feel this little lift through the tiller for a moment as the item slid under the rudder. Once it cleared, the rudder would drop back down where it belonged. This up-and-down travel was no more than two inches. In a floating-debris scenario, once past the object, you just wiggle the rudder a couple of times to make sure nothing is hung up on it and away you go. This time when I tried to wiggle the rudder, I couldn't move it. We were aground, and we were aground hard—the full length of the boat.

### Knowledge Nook

*Now normally you try to run with your bow heavy and at least four inches deeper in the water than the rest of the boat. Then if you run up on a sandbar, only the bow is stuck. You can then usually back off and find another route in deeper water without too much difficulty. This bow-heavy concept has a few drawbacks, but generally is better than getting grounded like we were. The drawbacks are that with the bow deeper than the rest of the craft, the steering is a little trickier because it changes the pivot point of the boat. It effectively moves it forward of the normal pivot point, thus making the steering more sensitive. Every boat has a certain point along its length on which it pivots when the rudder is turned. That point will change as the boat's load is shifted, or its draft is changed.*

*This is usually not an issue and can be easily compensated for with a little practice. This bow-heavy concept works great going upstream and is absolutely necessary going downstream, as you are usually moving much faster, and you also have the speed of the water pushing you along. So with all that momentum, you could get shoved way up on a sandbar if you didn't have that lowered bow protecting you. However, there is one very ugly side-effect to this downstream scenario.*

*All of a sudden that monster of all reversals appears and takes over, often wrenching the tiller from your grip. You see, it works like this…you're running downstream somewhat faster than the water is flowing, because if you don't, you have no steering. Remember our conversation about water running past the rudder for it to work? Now you have ground to a halt, and the water has stopped flowing past it from front to back. But the water has not stopped flowing. It has only stopped going the direction past your rudder you want it too. Now in an instant, the water is running past the rudder from rear to front. Instantly left becomes right and vice versa.*

*The other aspect of this backwards situation is that your pivot point for your boat has now moved to the very front. In addition, the rudder, which sticks out behind the rudder shaft (or hinges) attaching it to your boat, is being attacked from the rear with the moving water. This changes all the dynamics concerning rudder operation dramatically. If you're curious about just how much these dynamics are changed, take your old trusty yardstick outside on a windy day. With your back to the wind, hold the yardstick out and see how the wind affects it. Now turn around to face the wind and repeat the test; you will see what I mean when I say it changes the dynamics dramatically. The pressure applied to the tiller is tenfold what it is in normal operation, and it takes a very strong individual to keep the rudder under control. Most cannot do it for long, as they will overcompensate just a little, and the water will rip it out of their grip. When this happens, the boat will immediately begin to wheel one way or another and will get washed onto the sandbar sideways. Soon the sand will begin to wash away, and if you don't get the boat off quickly, you will become entombed permanently!*

## Now, where were we?

Oh, yes, aground, and aground hard. None of this was happening this time as we were stuck along the entire keel. Why? Because we were lazy and cocky, and when you get that way on the Missouri, she will jump out and bite you hard! It's like turning your back on a pet rattlesnake. **Bruce and Mike knew immediately what the problem was and jumped over to see how bad it was. They were in about twelve inches of water, and *Best Friend* draws about fourteen inches; it was bad indeed.** Bruce got up on the

cabin and checked out the river below us. With his years of experience reading this old girl, he calculated we were about one hundred fifty feet from deep water. We decided that the best move was to lift her stern a bit and let the hydraulic action of the water wash the sand from under her keel. Then we would rock her a bit and shove her ahead about two or three feet. It took us about three hours to get off that bar. There were about six of us actually lifting and shoving this twelve-ton boat.

Remember the last Knowledge Nook? Lewis and his men did the same thing, so they did indeed lift the boat. Now do you realize that Captain Lewis was literal in his writings? Some believe that Captain Lewis and his men could *not* have lifted the craft as he stated in his journals. And I say, "Of course they *couldn't have*...on dry ground in a *dead lift*." But they were in the water and were reducing buoyancy, which is quite different from a dead lift off dry ground.

While we were lifting and shoving, some of the college kids were out scraping a channel ahead of the keel in the sandbar with their feet. You simply draw an imaginary line out from the keel, which will normally be four to six inches wide, and start loosening the sand, and the river will do the rest. You may wonder why just a line in the sand for the keel. It protrudes below the hull specifically for this reason on a rivercraft. Now you can see that Lewis's men were not digging an eight-foot-wide trench, but rather a foot or so to accommodate only the keel. This task could be done by judgment and guessing and also with primitive tools or human feet!

As we approached the deep water line, Bruce said I should get back onboard. This "deep water" line is nothing more than an almost un-discernable disturbance in the water, which told experienced rivermen like Mike and Bruce just where the bottom dropped off. I was in the water, and could not see it as well as they could from the upper deck, although at the time I might very well not have known what I was seeing. I would now, but then I was yet a novice at some of this river wisdom.

Bruce was up on the boat and was looking down at this fine line, and he knew it was approaching fast. He hollered at me to take his hand and get aboard, and as I finally listened to his advice, I felt the sand disappear from beneath my feet. You see, the down-current sides of these bars are often deep holes the water has washed out over weeks, months, or even years. They can be twenty or more feet deep and often have a bunch of debris down in their belly. When an individual allows himself to be swept into one of them, it is like sliding down a water park water slide, but instead a fun splash at the end, you are entangled in a bunch of trees and stuff! This scenario usually ends in a drowning. I probably owe Bruce my life on that one. And thank you, Sir, again. I am amazed at just how many times I have come so close to buying the farm. I suspect when it finally happens, I will never see it coming.

**It was near dark, and we couldn't see a thing, so we snuggled up to a friendly sandbar and put up camp.** Mike Lange built us a one heck of a huge fire with driftwood, and we all had a very relaxing evening in the middle of the Missouri River, right in those footsteps of Lewis and Clark that everyone is always talking about.

Mike had a ten-pound beef roast. I still have no idea where he had been hiding that monster, but he rubbed it with his secret seasonings, wrapped it in about eight layers of tinfoil, and went ashore. I was curious, so I tagged along and watched as he and Bruce dug a deep hole very near the bonfire. Once completed, they shoveled in a bunch of the embers from the fire, dropped in the roast, shoveled in some more embers, and then filled the hole in with sand again. Mike turned to me and said that we would have supper in a few hours. Heck, it was 10:00 p.m. already, so I hit the sack. I found out in the morning that after a few drinks, the whole crew did. I figured that the roast was toast, but Mike dug it up in the morning, and we had roast beef for breakfast. It was perfectly done, as with no air it could not burn, and it was still warm. That boy is going to make some woman very happy some day, as she won't have to cook a single meal.

At the end of our stay at Camp Rheumatism, I entrusted *Best Friend* to the care of my newfound friends, as they were going to take her under power about six miles above Mandan and put her in a cove off the river near the town of Stanton, where they lived. Frank and I would come back and get her in the fall. I headed home to take care of business that was piling up.

As it turned out, it was later in the fall than we wanted before Frank and I went to retrieve *Best Friend*. By then we discovered that she had frozen in the ice of the cove, and if the expedition's accounts of the problems in the winter of 1805 were correct, I knew we were in for some work.

My new friends in North Dakota had expressed a desire to have a boat to run the river with that coming spring and had been asking me what it would cost to build a smaller one that could be hauled by a smaller truck. I told them about the *Raycliff*, and how she was no doubt ready to get her keel in the river again. It was settled. Frank and I would stop by Pierre on the way up and gather up *Raycliff* for them to use that next season on the upper Missouri.

I made arrangements with the science museum, and we headed for Pierre. I must admit, when I walked through those doors and saw the old girl for the first time in almost two years, I think she smiled as I laid my hand on her, and I know I shed a tear. We got her loaded and headed for Bismarck. Once there I said good-bye to her again, but promised that it would only be for one season. She was OK with that; after all, she would be back in her environment, the river.

It took two days of back-breaking labor to break enough ice to get *Best Friend* to the boat ramp, which was a mere sixty feet away. The guys who had helped us so much that summer offered to help us get *Best Friend* free of the ice and loaded when we got there. They deserved a reward! Once she was loaded Frank and I wasted no time getting home for the winter.

That winter, Catherine and I made another trip to Charlottesville. In the spring we launched *Best Friend* on Blue Lake at Lewis and Clark State Park back home in Iowa to be used as a floating educational tool by the Iowa Department of Natural Resources. That following fall, I went back to Stanton, North Dakota, and retrieved *Raycliff* and took her home. My nephew, Scott, joined me on this trip, and we had a great time! We launched her on Blue Lake as well, and from 2005 to 2006 she and *Best Friend* were berthed together at Lewis and Clark State Park.

**During this time we were invited to bring** *Raycliff* **down to Saint Louis to help them celebrate Independence Day, and to display her under the Saint Louis Arch!** When I told Frank I needed to take the old girl down and plant her near the Arch, he couldn't wait to get going. Once again we in-

vited some old friends along, offered to comp their rooms, and ended up having a great time! This was to be our last great adventure with *Raycliff*.

It was 2007. The bicentennial celebration of the Lewis and Clark Expedition was over, and the economy was crash-diving. We very sadly had to part with *Raycliff* and *Best Friend*. *Raycliff* went to a good home, and some-day I hope to see her again. *Best Friend* was sold to the Iowa Department of Natural Resources for permanent duty at Lewis and Clark State Park in Onawa as a living-history tool. I run her on the lake every summer.

In the six years since, we have had many major projects and hundreds of smaller ones. Our projects have ranged from rebuilding a replica Indian earth lodge and restoring log cabins to auto restorations and museum dis-play projects. I've also recently been working on this book.

I have already explained my answer to the question that folks have asked me since 1985: Why do you build wooden boats? Well, nowadays I feel that there are actually two parts to the answer, as building the boats has turned out to be only part of the equation. I've described the pure joy of building. But why do I program, teach, and share? I can explain it best with a short story.

Every June at the park, we have a festival celebrating the Lewis and Clark Expedition and the era of the mountain man, which closely followed in the footsteps of the Corps of Discovery, as Lewis called the men of the Lewis and Clark Expedition. One June in particular, it had been a long three-day event, and it was hot. I was beat, the crowds had gone, and it was time to close up *Best Friend* and go to dinner with some of my old Discovery Corps reen-actment group friends, whom I get to see about three times a year. One of those old friends, John Oien, was onboard, helping me tie the last of the lines to secure the boat so we could skip town. Down the dock came a lady with a young boy, maybe eight or nine years old. I turned to John and moaned under my breath. John said to me, "Oh, heck, it's just one more kid. It won't take long. Do the 'Indian thing,' He'll get a kick out of it." Now I should explain a couple of things to bring you up to speed on the "Indian thing." John works with pewter and makes, among other stuff, small replicas of the Lewis and Clark Expedition peace medals that they handed out to chiefs along the trail. The "Indian thing" that he is referring to is neat, although I'm not sure if it is historically accurate. Some say it is, and some say it's not. Anyway, as we understand it, if a Native American had wanted to show you something, he would lay it lay it in your upturned palm from his upturned palm. This indicates that he wants it back. If he had chosen to give it to you, he would turn his hand over and drop it into your hand. It was then a gift for you to keep.

I gave this boy and his mother a full tour of *Best Friend*. The boy was showing off his collection of stuff from the festival, which included a small token made of a feather and a fake bear claw the mountain men had been handing out. He obviously thought a lot of these, as he could not stop talking about them through my entire tour of the boat. Just before they left, I explained the "Indian thing" to them. Then I took a pewter peace medal from my pocket and laid it in the boy's hand palm up, and he remembered what I had told him, so after looking at it, he handed it back. I then handed it back to him; I dropped it into his hand, and his eyes lit up as he smiled from ear to ear. Then at his mother's urging, they hurried up the dock so we could get on with our departure. I turned to go when I heard a small voice holler out, "Hey, mister!" This little guy ran back down the dock and told me to hold out my hand. He then took his feather token and his bear claw he had been so proud of and dropped them into my hand. He then bounded off toward his mother, leaving me choking back tears, holding a bear claw and a feather (which I cherish to this day), and standing in disbelief that I had almost passed up the opportunity for this wonderful experience.

That chance encounter has touched my life forever, and I can only hope that it has given this little guy a life lesson about unselfish giving and new friendships. Two life lessons we can all use. Enough said on the subject of why we build these boats and share with others.

I hope you've enjoyed some of Catherine and my adventures and maybe gained some insight into what makes us tick. We have since built *Best Friend II*. She is more along the lines of the *Raycliff*, and we will use her for water-born engagements wherever requested. We still just love to do our living history programs, on the water whenever possible. Our weekend or sometimes weeklong programming excursions cost a lot, and unfortunately we can only do about one-tenth as many as we would like to. I want more and more to educate as many people as I possibly can before I am too old to do it any more, but funding has been tough to come by. I am nearing my sixty-seventh year, my forty-seventh year with my bride, Catherine. It's been a great run!...

Boy! I would really like to get out on that river one more time...

# Epilogue

It has been nearly two years since I finished writing this manuscript. Now that I am getting around to actually publishing it, I felt that an update was in order.

I have partially retired from programming at Lewis and Clark State Park. It was a forced partial retirement, but that's what you get when you butt heads with a large government organization. I recently found one of my report cards from my early school days. It states in no uncertain terms, "He does not play well with others." I guess some things never change.

Cathy and I are looking forward to the next decades if the Good Lord will give them to us. I always have projects in the wind, and will no doubt keep busy until I can do so no longer. My interest in pre-steam era rivercraft will never die, and I am always looking forward to the next crazy venture, be it floating or not.

Remember that young man who helped me build *Best Friend* back in 2004? Nathan Butler has turned into a very fine person and a close friend.

Other than that, I can only say this: "I sure would like to get back on the river again!"

# Some Background On the Author

## By His Daughter, Shari Lynn

My dad, "Butch" Bouvier aka "Mr. Keelboat," was born in 1947 to Alfred Clifton Bouvier Senior and Elsie Mae Bouvier. My grandparents had both worked at the Swan Island Shipyards in Portland, Oregon, during World War II, building T-2 Liberty Tankers. They had tried to have children for several years, but to no avail. They were fortunate to adopt a baby girl, my dad's older sister, Sandra. A few years later, they were surprised to find out that they were going to have a little boy! My dad, Alfred Clifton Bouvier Junior also ended up having a younger brother, Gary, and a younger sister, Rena.

When my dad was young, the family lived very well. My dad states it simply as, "My Father was a good provider." Well, I know that they lived (as my grandma would put it) pretty high off the hog! They had the first TV in the neighborhod and pretty much the best of everything that was new. I've heard many stories of the month-long trips that the family took visiting numerous states each summer. And vacations were most always camping trips. The family became quite the campers over the years! My dad and his siblings got to stay in some of the most beautiful areas in America. He can tell you of a trip where they pitched tent next to a beautiful rushing stream in Montana. He woke up to the sound of the stream as it wandered by the campsite. He has shared with me the feeling he experienced that morning and many others while camping, and has said they were quite remarkable.

One trip, which is now part of our family's lore, was in 1957. My grandpa had purchased a brand-new, burnt-orange Mercury station wagon. He had built a camping trailer for it and had painted it to match. The family piled in and headed for the new ALCAN Alaskan Highway for a three-month summer-long adventure. I remember stories of this trip so well because I have some food tins, snow-blindness goggles, and various items found at an abandoned mercantile store from the Gold Rush that my grandpa came across on that trip!

I treasure those items as well as other things that have been handed down to me. They all have such a rich history and tell so many stories of my family's adventures. I have large seashells and a glass float from a Japanese fisherman's net brought back from one of their West Coast trips. I have a giant pinecone from the Redwoods. And no, even though you could still drive through a huge cut-out redwood tree back then, they didn't get to because the luggage rack on the car that held all their camping gear and moose antlers wouldn't clear. (But I've seen pictures of the whole family standing in it!) My dad was fortunate as a child to have visited so many states. It must have been so enriching! My grandma told me when I was a little girl that she and my grandpa had been to every state except for Hawaii.

It's worth noting that the first camping trip they ever took paved the path for my dad to become a life-long Boy Scout. My grandpa had bought a brand-new fancy tent for their first camping adventure. I guess he had one heck of a time trying to set the thing up. Then this boy came along and helped my grandpa set it up and secure it in no time flat. My grandpa offered him some money for his kindness, but the boy refused. He told my grandpa it was his good deed for the day, and explained to him about Boy Scouts. My grandparents came back from that camping trip, and later that fall they started Pack 86. The irony of this is that the Boy Scouts of America started in the United States in the very same way. Of course that boy was in London in the year 1910, and his good deed was giving directions in a thick fog to a gentleman on a business trip, but nonetheless, the Boy Scouts of America exists today because of a good deed. And Pack 86 exists now because of another.

My dad loved being active in Boy Scouts. It was a very hands-on program with new things to learn. He had already graduated from drawing planes, boats, and cars to building models of them. He was always designing something and building it, or taking something apart to find out what made it work. He was fascinated with mechanical stuff and how it worked or why it didn't (which is why he was capable of a recent project: completely restoring my 1960 AMC Rambler station wagon…all the way down to rewinding the rheostat coil in the fuel level sender unit inside the fuel tank). He figured it out from a book, which is no surprise, as he has always read everything he could get his hands on. Research has always been his specialty.

My dad told me of the time when he was still really young and he had found an old hydraulic jack in the garage. He asked his dad what it did, and his dad explained that you could lift very heavy objects with it, and he showed my dad how it worked. Soon after, my grandpa left for work. During the course of that day, my dad had lifted the front porch, my grandma's car, my grandpa's tractor...you get the picture.

Model rockets captured his interest as he got older. He designed one model rocket with a super-powered, homemade "rocket boost system." When this system was in its infancy stages, my dad said it smoked a lot. So when he was testing the completed model, he said he had located himself far enough away from the smoke he was expecting by connecting some wires hooked to an igniter he had rigged from a glow plug that he had stripped off of a spare model airplane. Thank God he did that, because his rocket boost system (aka pipe bomb) blew up the back half of my grandpa's garage. Oh, boy, I heard grandpa was hot over that one! It's a wonder how my grandparents actually survived my dad's youth.

I bet by keeping him busy and putting him to work. My grandpa had been a contractor, and my dad had worked many summers for him. My dad told me once, "When you mix mud by hand, and tend block for Dad and Uncle Lester for twelve hours, you know you have worked!" My Dad said that my grandpa taught by example, and when he thought you were ready to "fly by yourself," he would say something like, "your cat, you skin it," and walk away. My dad looks back upon this as an effective teaching method. He says it shows if one "has the metal or not."

My grandpa was a contractor and new-home speculator/builder. Back when my dad was younger, my grandpa had purchased about twenty-seven acres of property in Council Bluffs. It had an old barn standing on it, which he planned to remodel into a "summer" home for the family. And good thing he had done that, because in the summer of 1965, after years of success, my grandpa was forced into bankruptcy. The housing market had been negatively influenced by some new controversial regulations that slowed and practically halted the purchase of homes in the area. My grandpa had been doing extremely well at the time, and therefore happened to be sitting on a whole slug of new houses and properties when the market came to a screeching and unexpected halt.

My grandpa lost everything, except that old barn house and the acreage in Council Bluffs. My dad went from being a junior at Benson High in Omaha to starting his senior year at Thomas Jefferson High in Council Bluffs. My dad has told me that my grandpa's bankruptcy was pretty tough on the family, although his parents seemed to take it in stride. He told me recently that since his parents were both survivors of The Great Depression, they knew "how to be broke." Dad says that knowing how to be broke is the first step to becoming un-broke. Also, in hindsight, my dad is convinced that quite possibly suddenly being poor was the best thing that ever happened to him. You see, up until that point in his life, my dad had been somewhat of a silver-spooned brat who thought money grew on trees. He had the best of the best bikes, toys, and gadgets. And he had always enjoyed his own private bedroom and bathroom. Reality check! He went from that to using an outhouse virtually overnight!

He has told me that he would hate to think how he would have turned out without that little "awakening." Picture this: Grandma and Grandpa had just bought my dad a top-of-the-line, green-and-white Benson letter jacket at the end of his junior year. My dad (whose decisions weren't always filled with wisdom back then) decided to wear his fancy new green-and-white jacket to his new school, whose colors were orange and black. Talk about standing out in a crowd! He learned how to fight that year. And he still has the jacket, bloodstains and all!

It was evident to my dad that my grandma and grandpa were financially having a tough time. My grandpa worked for his brother and was also starting to do some independent contracting again. My dad went to work every night after high school at a packing plant. And unlike children today, he gave a large portion of his earnings to his parents. Of course, he just brushes this off by saying, "That's just what you did back then." Anyway, within a few years, my grandpa had pulled himself back out of debt and was on top again. He had started subdividing the acreage into lots, building on them, and selling them. Bouvier Acres is still around. A road named Bouvier Lane services it. Quite an accomplishment for my grandpa who was a fifty-eight-year-old man at the time!

Around that same time, my dad met his future bride, Catherine Kern, at an Easter sunrise service. He did not know then that she was to become his best friend and confidante. They dated for several years, and then decided to get married. Their original wedding date was moved up because my dad had enlisted in the service (Why not? Everyone was being drafted anyway.), and he would need to leave for boot camp. So they married on December 2, 1966. My dad served his term in the United States Army, and after his enlistment was up, he came home to be with his sweetheart, who had given birth to their first daughter, Wendy Sue, in July 1969. I was born in December 1970.

My dad tells me that he went through various jobs early in their marriage. He was always taking charge on each job, which as often as not annoyed his employer. One of his bosses gave him the suggestion once that if he wanted to be in charge all the time, then maybe he should start his own business. So he did! My mom and dad purchased about five hundred dollars worth of Craftsman tools. And since he loved working on cars, he opened up A.C.'s Tune-Up Shop in a one-car garage with a dirt floor. The tune-up business left a lot to be desired in those early days.

He told me about the day that he was at a car lot in Omaha, trying to round up some tune-up work. The owner of the lot asked my dad if he did any auto body work. My dad responded, "You bet!" The owner instructed him to take an old Cadillac back with him and patch all the rust in it. So my dad left his old Chevy pickup at the car lot and drove the junk Cadillac straight to the Council Bluffs library, where he checked out a book on how to do auto body work. He then took the Caddy to his one-car garage and repaired it. He says he's sure it wasn't his best job ever, but the car was repaired, and it looked nice. My dad found himself changing professions, and A.C.'s Body Shop was born.

For the next sixteen years, my dad did auto body work and repair. He has been featured in Hot Rod Magazine four times and has also taken top honors at car shows. That was nice, but even nicer to him was that his work paid the mortgage on the house and fed our family.

One thing I do remember distinctly as a young girl is that my dad was always active in Boy Scouting. When my sister and I were still young, my dad became the leader of Troop 86. Of course my mom was right there helping out too. She also found the time for my and my sister's Brownie troop. (In fact, I am positive that if she never has to sew another badge on a uniform in her life, she'll not mind one lick!)

My dad holds the Scouter's Key. He is a Vigil member of the Order of the Arrow. His Indian name is NUJUDUM, which means, "He who carries the load." He is both a Founders Award and Silver Beaver recipient. He also went through Wood Badge leadership training. None of that, though, could replace what my dad heard at an airport several years back while waiting for his sister and my mom to return from a week vacation to Las Vegas. He had gone to the airport with two roses to greet them, an inside joke between him and his sister. This young army captain named Troy (who had been my dad's OA ceremony team leader) recognized him while checking for arrivals. He'd not seen my dad for many years. They instantly gave each other a big hug, and spoke for a few minutes. Trying to catch up on fifteen years in fifteen minutes was an impossible task. Troy had to leave, as his fiancée was arriving at another gate, so they said their good-byes, and Troy turned to leave. About five feet away, he turned back around and said, "Butch, I just want to tell you what a positive influence you were on my life. Thank you!" He then turned and hurried off. Boy! My mom and my aunt Sandra sure must have thought that my dad had missed them tremendously while they were gone because as they walked in, Troy had just left, and there stood my dad with a rose for each of them and tears in his eyes.

When my sister and I were a little older, my dad decided to take his woodworking hobby he enjoyed so much and make it a business. He closed A.C.'s Body Shop, and the next week "Bouvier Construction" was proudly emblazoned on the sides of his 1954 Chevy pickup. He had always done woodworking on the side for as long as I can remember. He's done leatherwork, blacksmithing, and 1800s woodwright type woodworking. I remember going with him to trade and craft shows to demo stuff like a treadle-powered wood lathe or a shaving horse and draw knives. We all just had a ball!

Of course my dad naturally fell into building wooden boats. Shortly after my sister and I were out of high school, his hobby began to grow into an obsession, and in the year 2000 his new career of historical boatbuilding took off with his new company, L&C Replicas. And little did we all know then the adventures that lay ahead.

*–My dad's number one fan,*
*Shari Lynn Bouvier Keefe*

# Glossary

*We sent out copies of the book to different groups for proofreading and suggestions. We asked if they wanted us to define any terms or words. The following glossary is a result of their comments.*

**A-frames:** *Butch Bouvier*
In my world, A-frames are no more than giant sawhorses. Often when I have to lift a large boat, I will build them with telephone poles, and they will measure twelve to fourteen feet tall, and that distance or more wide.

**Ballast:** *The Mariner's Dictionary*
A quantity of iron, stone, gravel, or other weighty substance in the lower hold of a vessel, or in some cases metal bolted to the keel, to increase stability by lowering the center of gravity.

**Beam:** *The Mariner's Dictionary*
A thwartship timber or member of a vessel upon which the decks are laid.
*Butch Bouvier*
For all intents and purposes, when someone talks about a ship's beam they are referring to how wide it is.

**Block and Tackle:** *Webster's New World Dictionary*
Pulley blocks and ropes or cables, used for hoisting large heavy objects.

**Capsizing:** *The Mariner's Dictionary*
To turn over.

**Carpe diem:** *Webster's New World Dictionary*
Seize the day / make the most of the day

**Chine:** *The Mariner's Dictionary*
The line of intersection between the sides and bottom of a flat-bottomed boat.

**Chip log and how a ship's knots is figured:** *The Mariner's Dictionary*
A device that consists of a wooden quadrant about five inches in radius with lead placed in the circular edge, which causes it to float upright. It is made

fast to a log line by a three-part bridle. The part fitted to the upper corner is slightly shorter than the other two parts of the bridal and has a socket and a pin that pulls out when a strain is placed upon it. The chip is then easily hauled aboard. The chip is cast over (streamed) with the pin in position. The first fifteen or thirty fathoms of line is called the *stray line,* which is marked by a piece of red bunting. The line from this point is divided into parts of 47 feet 3 inches. Each part is called a knot. They are marked by pieces of cord tucked through the strands with knots in their ends corresponding to the number of knots out. Each knot is subdivided into fifths and marked with a white rag. The log is allowed to run out while a twenty-eight second glass is emptying itself. The result is the rate of speed of the vessel. The length of the knot was derived from the proportion that one hour (3600 seconds) is to 28 seconds as one mile (6080 feet) is to the length of a knot (47 feet, 3 inches).

**Coefficients of drag:** *Science Digest*
In fluid dynamics, the drag coefficient (commonly denoted as: cd, cx or cw) is a dimensionless quantity that is used to quantify the drag or resistance of an object in a fluid environment such as air or water.
*Butch Bouvier*
The amount of resistance that water has as it flows past the hull of a ship reduced to an equation that can then be used in other formulas. This information helps engineers in hull design versus required power to move ships through water at a given speed.

**Come-along:** *Butch Bouvier*
A mechanical device consisting of a drum in a steel frame, which is wound with a steel cable. There is a hook at both ends and a handle, which when worked will ratchet on a tooth system on the drum and will apply over 2,000 pounds of pressure on the two hooks.

**Cordelle:** *Early American Rivers*
A cordelle is defined as a twisted cord or tassel. It is a towrope, especially that was formerly used on Mississippi flatboats and keelboats. This word can also refer to the act of towing with a cordelle.

**Dead rise:** *The Mariner's Dictionary*
The rise of a floor of a vessel above the horizontal. It is the rise of the sides of a vessel's bottom above the base line at the intersection with the molded breadth line.

**Displacement:** *The Mariner's Dictionary*
The weight of the water displaced by a vessel, equal to the weight of the vessel.

**Draft:** *The Mariner's Dictionary*
The depth of water necessary to float a vessel.

**Fasteners:** *Butch Bouvier*
Those items, metal or wood, used to fasten one piece of wood to another.

**Flat boats:** *The Mariner's Dictionary*
A scow-shaped vessel of shallow draft, mostly used in river work.

**Frames:** *The Mariner's Dictionary*
The skeleton structure of a vessel.

**Handy man jack:** *Butch Bouvier*
A simple high-lifting mechanical jack, which will lift about 900 pounds to a height of about 2 1/2 feet. All mechanical with pins that walk up a perforated steel shaft.

**John boat:** *The Mariner's Dictionary*
A small pulling boat, adaptable for outboard; square at bow and stern. Used as a tender or for hunting and fishing.

**Keel:** *The Mariner's Dictionary*
The backbone of a vessel from which rises the frames or ribs.

**Linseed oil:** *Webster's New World Dictionary*
A yellowish oil extracted from flax seed used in oil paints, etc.

**Longhorns:** *Butch Bouvier*
A nickname given some homemade downriver flat boats in the early 1800s. They were fitted with very long oars on the sides, as well as the bow and stern for some control no matter which direction they were turned. Evidently the long oars protruding over their sides reminded some of the horns of animals.

**Mackinaw boat:** *Butch Bouvier*
A term loosely used to describe a variety of smaller, shallow-draft craft used on inland waterways in the early 1800s.

**Mooring bitt:** *Mariner's Dictionary*
A pair or single iron or wooden head set vertically to which mooring or tow lines are made fast.
**Pirogue:** *Butch Bouvier*

A term loosely used to describe small inland waterway craft; often dugouts and small canoe type craft, but sometimes larger craft. Generally understood today as a double-ended, flat-bottomed canoe type craft about twenty feet long and very common in southern swamps.

**Pit saw:** *Webster's New World Dictionary*
A large saw with handles at each end, used in a vertical position by two people, one standing above the timber to be cut, the other in a pit below it.

**Plank on frame:** *Butch Bouvier*
In this construction technique, the frame or skeleton of the craft is built first, and then planks are attached to it.

**Portage:** *Webster's New World Dictionary*
The carrying of boats or supplies overland between navigable rivers, lakes, or other bodies of water.

**Pressure-treated lumber:** *Woodworking Magazine*
Wood that has had a liquid preservative forced into it in order to protect against deterioration due to rot or insect attack. The most commonly used preservatives are chromated copper arsenate.

**Pre-steam era:** *Butch Bouvier*
The period of time before the advent of the steam-powered rivercraft. It extended into that steam era about forty years, ending about 1870.

**Reefed sail:** *Butch Bouvier*
When a sail is not being used, it will be tied tightly to the yard or boom to keep it from flailing around in the wind.

**Reynolds number:** *The Chemical Engineer's handbook*
In fluid mechanics, the Reynolds number (Re) is a dimensionless quantity that gives a measure of the ratio of inertial forces to viscous forces and consequently quantifies the relative importance of these two types of forces for given flow conditions.

**Rosetta Stone:** *Internet Encyclopedia*
An ancient Egyptian granodiorite stele inscribed with a decree issued at Memphis in 196 BC on behalf of King Ptolemy V. The decree appears in three scripts: the upper text is Ancient Egyptian hieroglyphs, the middle portion Demotic script, and the lowest Ancient Greek. Because it presents essentially the same text in all three scripts (with some minor differences

among them), it provided the key to the modern understanding of Egyptian hieroglyphs.

**Scantlings:** *The Mariner's Dictionary*
The dimensions of frames, girders, stringers, plating, and planking that form a ship's structure.

**Skiff:** *The Mariner's Dictionary*
A small, light rowing boat.

**Socratic:** *Webster's New World Dictionary*
A method of teaching, as used by Socrates, in which a series of questions leads the answerer to a logical conclusion.

**Steering oar:** *The Mariner's Dictionary*
A long oar used as a rudder.

**Sweep:** *Butch Bouvier*
A large and long rudder fitted to the boat on a U-joint so it can be lifted in and out of the water as well as from side to side.

**Thole pin:** *The Mariner's Dictionary*
Wooden pin that fits up in the rail or gunnel of a boat to hold the oars and provide a pivot point for their use.

**Tiller:** *The Mariner's Dictionary*
A bar of iron or wood connected with the rudder head and leading usually forward. By the tiller, the rudder is moved as desired.

**Trolling motor:** Butch Bouvier
A form of boat motor powered by a 12-volt battery.

**Turpentine:** *Webster's New World Dictionary*
A light-colored volatile oil distilled from such oleoresins, used in paints and varnishes.

**Wet well:** *Butch Bouvier*
An opening in the hull of a boat to allow an outboard motor to be lowered into it.

**Yard:** *The Mariner's Dictionary*
A spar crossing a mast horizontally from which a square sail is set.

# Building Raycliff

*Larry cutting screws that came through sheeting*

*Carolyn caulking joints*

*Mike spreading glue on 5/4-inch planks before installation*

*Larry and Gary nursing her into dock for the first time just after launch at Blue Lake*

*Interior shot showing below-deck framing and flotation sheets*

*Gary programming at Lynch*

# Triumphant Return

*Robbie*

*"Doc" & Nate*

*Taking her out for a portage*

*Programming aboard at Springfield*

*First day just below
Fort Randall Dam*

*Under full sail*

*My crew at Lynch*

*Coming up a narrow
and shallow chute*

*Dale and Corporal,
aka Frank Koeppe*

*Frank and Mike practicing*

*First sail just below
Fort Randall Dam*

*Last day on the water
at Sioux City docks*

*My crew working Raycliff around an outcropping*

*Raycliff coming up the chute at Sunshine Bottom*

*Gary teaching sextant navigation*

*A full boat at Elk Point*

*Elk Point landing*

*Nathan helping with a program*

*Our wonderful bow cannon*

*Dale holding class*

*Dale and Butch*

*Everyone's ashore at Springfield*

*Just before the skinny-dipping at Fort Randall. That's Doc playing in the water, go figure.*

*Willard and his small boat, hard at work as usual*

*Not sure where, but a pretty picutre, to be sure!*

*My wild bunch!*

*Two of my favorite pictures of Raycliff*

# Bismarck Parks

*After building the keelboat, Frank took her up to Bismarck for me.*

*The cranes sat her in position, and I would come up later and finish her.*

*Completed, she is sitting in a fiberglass lake. The first visitors really enjoyed her.*

*The beginnings of the steam boat in Onawa*

*Hull completed, awaiting upper decks*

*Upper decks coming together*

*Complete and ready to be disassembled and shipped to Bismarck*

*Reassembled and sitting along
the Missouri in Bismarck*

*Some of the first visitors
on the weather deck*

*The front half of the steamboat Yellowstone complete with rigging,
grasshopper rig, and boiler*

# Best Friend Build

*The hull is "in frame" here*

*Keel first*

*Bottom painted and ready for the hull to be turned over*

*Finishing the plywood covering*

*Just over, now we can get to work planking over the plywood with 5/4-inch thick by 6-inch-wide cedar.*

*She looked good with her cedar planking,
but once varnished she was a beauty!*

*Next I frame up the cabin.*

*Once framed, I wasted no time getting it sheeted and planked.*

*Then I turned my attention to the final details.*

*Name plates and cannon in place*

*Mike Butler brings me a gift.*

*To get her out of the building, we had to remove one of the walls.*

*My loading crew: Mandy Koeppe, me, Vicki and Frank Koeppe, Nathan Butler, Danny, and a spectator*

# Fort Calhoun

*Just before Best Friend left for her Bismarck adventure, she made a couple of special appearances. The first was before she was actually completed in Hartford, Illinois. The second was to be at another signature event in Fort Calhoun, Nebraska.*

*Dr. Gary Moulton was onboard.*

*Some folks from the US mint*

*And an armored car full of brand-new Keelboat nickels for a first day release*

*Then-Nebraska lieutenant governor, Dave Heineman, presented me with a special award.*

*We topped off our banner day with some very colorful Native Americans.*

# Camp Rheumatism

*Best Friend approaching the chute near Camp Rheumatism*

*Best Friend at Camp Rheumatism dock*

*Showing a young visitor how to fire a cap-lock pistol*

*Getting the old girl off the mud after a river level drop overnight*

*Drinking wine and playing movie director*

*One of our many beautiful sunsets on the upper Missouri*

*Ominous storm clouds brewing at sunset*